POSITIVELY DISNEY

POSITIVELY DISNEY

MORE HEARTWARMING STORIES ABOUT DISNEY'S IMPACT ON PEOPLE'S LIVES

KIMBERLEY BOUCHARD

ISBN: 0692892354
ISBN 13: 9780692892350
Library of Congress Control Number: 2017907837
New Oak Publishing, Newcastle, WA

I would like to dedicate this book to my parents Gladys and Florian Borstmayer, who first introduced me to the magic in our living room with The Wonderful World of Disney on Sunday nights.

Acknowledgements   ix
Introduction   xi

A Royal Proposal   1
With a Little Help From our Friends   7
A Friendship Forged   13
Double Acts of Kindness   20
Marathon Man   26
My Goofy   35
The Art of Life   40
Happiness by Chance   48
Special Affects   54
Power Princess   61
Tsum Tsums with Heart   69
Toni's Time   75
Dora's Dream   80
Walking Warrior   84
Living the Dream   96

Something Disney   103
Just Dance   111
The Ministry of Disney   118
You've Got a Friend in Me   126
Seeing Mickey   134
The Real Princess Tiana   141
Disney Dreams for Everyone   146
A Hope and a Dream   152
Ms. Incredible   157
Snow White's Gift   162
Thank You   169
Disney Sisters   178
The Collector   184
Misadventure   189
The Disney Connection   198
Gaston's Little Belle   205
The Gift of Goofy, the Magic of Mickey   211

Afterword   219
Contributors   221
About the Author   223

ACKNOWLEDGEMENTS

IT NEVER CEASES TO AMAZE me, the kindness of all the wonderful people I have been blessed to meet while collecting stories for this series. I would like to thank every one of you who took time out of your busy life to share your story with me. It has been both a pleasure and a privilege to write them.

I would like to thank the following people whose stories are a part of this second book in the Positively Disney series: Jennifer Baldovinos, Joe Bell, Cheryl Biazzo, Joe Biazzo, Angelica Doria, Mike Flynn, Abigail Forrest, Timothy Gill, Fr. George Gulash, Dan Hartley, Mikey Jacobs, Kevin-John Jobczynski, Emmaline Johnson, Geoffrey Kanner, Mell Mallin, Lisa Matters, Yesenia McCoy, Kylee McGrane, Kaley McLean, Brenden McNeil, Lou Mongello, Diane Myers, Emma Jane Napier, Andy Attwood Otto, Marissa Parks, Roberto Romero, Basilio Santana, Sara Slade, Sophie Slade, Toni Campitiello Smith, Dora Speck, Nataly Pacifico White, Amy Wyand, Michelle Young, Mike Zevon.

To see the photographs that go along with these stories, please visit the gallery at www.positivelydisney.com.

I would like to thank my friends and family for listening to me share some of these stories and being there for me in my time of need. I would like to particularly thank Father George Gulash, my friend, confidant, and fellow Disney lover for the lovely chats; my mom who always listened to a story that I wanted to share; my children Alexis, Christophe, and Tristan for being at the ready when I needed you; and my husband, Jacques, who has been at my side and my biggest fan from the beginning. I love you all, and all of you have made me a better person.

Thank you.

INTRODUCTION

DISNEY SPEAKS TO THE HEARTS of fans everywhere. It envelopes universal truths of humanity really, and delivers them back to people everywhere in the form of the Disney magic. We all want acknowledgement, need unconditional acceptance, desire joy, want peace in our hearts, and to feel loved. And isn't this how we all feel when we walk through those park gates? We are acknowledged from the moment we walk in to the moment that we depart at the end of the day with a wave good bye from giant Mickey gloves. We are accepted and welcomed no matter who we are or where we have come from.

We matter, and it shows through the world-class service provided to thousands of us throughout our stay. We experience the joy of being a kid again where we can simply play and enjoy ourselves wearing our Disney shirts, costumes, and Mickey ears. We can find peace in our hearts in this magical world and leave our worries behind, if only for a short while. We can be carefree and live in the present with our friends and our families on Disney time.

Even though I have been blessed to have visited Walt Disney World too many times to count, I still experience the magic. During Christmas 2016, my family and I re-experienced Mickey's Merry Christmas Party and the beautiful processional that we hadn't done for over a decade. It was like experiencing it for the first time and it was wonderful. We got to see the drone show at Disney Springs and although short, it was epic with its hundreds of drones moving and lighting up the sky to holiday music.

I got to meet the Mariachi Cobre (see book 1: Hayden and the Mariachi Cobre). It was really special to meet some of the founding members who have been doing the shows for the last 34 years. I also thoroughly enjoyed meeting up with some contributors to book 1 and 2 as well. What was initially meant to be a 90-minute meetup for coffee turned into three hours of great fun talking and sharing! A surprise dinner with Kevin-John, whose story is in this book, ended with him presenting me with a painting that my husband had commissioned. I was in absolute tears over it; it is Donald Duck (my guy), sitting on the beach reading my book. It was such a surprise and a pleasure getting to know him and his lovely girlfriend.

A couple of magical moments happened within my family as well. After being caught in a sudden rainstorm while shopping at The Meadow Trading Post at Fort Wilderness Resort, my teenage son Christophe and I improvised rain coats out of the largest Disney gift bags in the store. Popping our heads through a slit at the bottom, we ran out the door, him carrying a gift bag while wearing one himself, and I wearing one that only exposed my head and legs. Dodging puddles, we laughed at how ridiculous our situation had become. We were a sight to see! We looked like two runaway gift bags from the store. It was then that we heard a little voice pipe up from the bus shelter. "Look Mommy! They're wearing Disney gift bags!" At this we roared, laughing and prancing through puddles all the way back to our RV. What a glorious belly chuckle that was, shared with my son, on a rainy winter Florida night. A magic moment of such childlike fun that we could share together. And of course, it happened at Disney, the most magical place on earth.

I hope you enjoy this second book as much as I enjoyed writing it!

Peace and Pixie Dust,
Kimberley

A ROYAL PROPOSAL

*"I especially loved Disney – I loved the princesses. Belle is
the best to me. She is intelligent and sets a great example."*

— KALEY MCLEAN

"I wanted to do something spectacular."

— BRENDEN MC NEIL

HAVE YOU EVER WONDERED WHAT the next sequence of the story
might be after the prince and princess finally get together?
How do they get to the "they lived happily ever after" part?
That next segment, the royal proposal, gets performed for
real in the final scene of one of my favourite Disney stories:
Beauty and the Beast. Several hundred people were privy to the
live proposal to Belle, aka Kaley McLean, from her transformed prince, aka Brenden McNeil, one Sunday afternoon

in October 2016. To say Kaley was surprised would be an understatement.

Both Brenden and Kaley grew up in the Florida area and still reside there, a mere 40 minutes from Walt Disney World. They were high school sweethearts, meeting five months before the end of their senior year when their English teacher placed them in the same small group. Kaley loved Disney growing up, especially the princesses; she dressed up as one every Halloween. She also did theatre throughout her school life, but she was never fortunate enough to be a princess in any of her productions.

One day, Kaley's dad came upon an announcement that a local theatre was auditioning for a new production. It was *Beauty and the Beast.* Even though Kaley hadn't done theatre for about five years, her dad encouraged her to try out for the part of Belle, her favourite princess. "She's very intelligent and she sets a great example [for young girls]" Kaley told me. Her family thought that she would make a great Belle.

And as we all know, she landed that coveted princess role. "The entire experience was really fun because I hadn't done it in a very long time. It brought me back to the good old theatre days." It required two months of rehearsal for the two weekends of performances, six in all. This would be a lot of work as Kaley was holding down a full-time job at the same time.

Brenden was musically inclined himself. However, he had never had any experience with theatre "or paid attention to that whole realm before," he says. It was Kaley who brought him into it and he quite enjoys it now.

The production was into its first two weeks of rehearsals in August 2016 when Brenden, his best friend, and his best friend's dad were having dinner one day. Brenden told them that he wanted to do something spectacular when he proposed to Kaley. His friend's dad nonchalantly suggested, "Well, why don't you just be the prince?" referring to the production that Kaley was doing. Brenden paused and thought *Wait a second! This is actually a really good idea!* From that moment forward, Brenden started formulating the plan to propose to Kaley on stage.

They had already talked a lot about the idea of marriage, "to ensure you're both on the same page, to gauge where the person is at," he says. But that is as far as it had gone. The first thing Brenden did was ask Kaley's dad for permission. The next step was to reach out to the director herself. Lucky for him, Kaley's dad knew the director. He helped Brenden connect with her, and Brendan sent her a two-page letter about who he was and why and what his proposal was going to be. Basically, "begging her to just let me kind of interrupt her play," Brenden says. Lucky for him, she loved sappy endings and enthusiastically agreed, much to Brenden's relief.

However, he was going to get only *one* practice due to their very tight schedule. A date and time was set.

To Brenden's dismay, it turned out that he was to practice the same time Kaley would be in practice that day. "This was quite nerve wracking" he shares. To help keep the secret, he found parking away from the theatre and snuck in the back door.

Brenden did a quick rehearsal while his brother filmed it. This way, he would be able to study the scene on his own and Brenden's brother could then add the footage to the rest of the recording of the actual proposal afterwards as well. He had just finished practicing when some of the cast started entering the room. Taken by surprise, Brenden took off out of the room. He had to get out of there quickly before Kaley came in!

During this last week of rehearsal, the cast could finally focus on the last scene which was the waltz scene. Kaley was getting "a little freaked out" at the time constraints Brenden said. She had not only a duet to perform but the waltz with the prince as well. This was a perfect opportunity for Brenden to help her out. He suggested that she teach him the waltz. This way she would feel more confident knowing it, and Brenden could learn it too.

Kaley jumped at the idea and started teaching Brenden. "That part was kind of cool," Brenden admits. It took Brenden a while to get the footing correct. Kaley assured him that he really didn't have to learn the whole thing. Now it was Brenden's turn "to freak out a bit." He insisted that he wanted to learn the whole thing, *he had to learn the whole thing.*

That final week, with the anticipation of the public proposal and all it entailed on stage made Brenden a little quiet and edgy. He brushed off Kaley's concern as "just stuff going on at work."

The day finally arrived. It was the Sunday of the first weekend of performances. It was show time for Brenden. "I woke up in a really good mood – overwhelmingly happy." He was relaxed the whole day, even sneaking behind the scenes. He didn't get the slightest bit nervous until his brother, who was standing behind him filming as he was about to go on, placed his hand on Brenden's shoulder. And that hand was trembling. His *brother* was nervous.

Initially, Brenden was supposed to walk down the steps to the stage at the same time as Kaley on the other side. However, the director thought that it may be a bit hazardous for Kaley to walk down the steps after seeing Brenden at the top. So she had Brenden wait for her to reach the bottom of the stairs before he ran down them to meet her. He had to descend quickly so as not to miss his cue. It looked to Kaley that she was going to have to carry on without the prince. "When I looked across and no one was there, I just thought the guy playing the prince had missed his cue," Kaley said. She was thinking *Okay, I'm going to go down there and do a solo.* "The director had made a strong point that whatever happens, to just keep going."

Kaley was just about to start singing when she looked up and saw Brenden flying down the stairs. "I'm instantly confused," she said. "I'm all ready to start singing and he comes out. I start singing anyways but I wasn't too confident on my feet because I was still pretty confused." The song begins with a question and Brenden began singing the harmony. *What was going on? Brenden seemed to know what he was doing,* Kaley wondered.

They continued walking down the steps doing the duet. Kaley believed that they were just going to continue down the steps and finish the play when suddenly, Brenden stopped.

"Everything kind of went quiet and the audience started murmuring," Brenden said. A good portion of the audience had no idea what was going on. The ones who did know were friends and family and some others that had gotten wind that something special was going to take place during the matinee performance. It had sold out because of this. Kaley's family had flown in for the show. She merely thought that because she hadn't done theatre for a while that they were just excited to see it. It wasn't unusual for her family to do something like this she says. Kaley was both right and wrong.

"Oh, my god! No way," someone was heard saying. The rest of the audience finally caught on as Brenden, with his princess, proposed to Kaley in front of nearly 400 people that afternoon.

"It was just incredible," Kaley said. The entire audience stood up and cheered. And then they continued with the rest of the show. Kaley knew that Brenden knew the waltz because she was the one who had taught it to him. *Ahhh,* she could see now. And all the pieces started to fall into place.

And this is what the next scene between Belle and her prince looked like that day in a little theatre packed with those who still believed in happily ever afters.

ꞶITH A LITTLE HELP FROM ꝊUR FRIENDS

*"If I've got people fighting for me, then
I've got to fight for me as well."*

—JOE BIAZZO

*"He couldn't believe all the responses, not just
cards, but gifts. And we gained new friends."*

— CHERYL BIAZZO

I HAVE WITNESSED THE LOYALTY of fans, as I and my family are among them. I have also seen and heard about the warmth and kindness of Disney fans as guests and cast members. But the compassion and kindness shown to the couple in their time of need in my next story by the Disney Facebook groups called "Diehard Disney Nuts, You Might be a Disney Addict If, and Walt Disney World Insiders" made me love this community of Disney goodness even more.

Joe and Cheryl Biazzo had both visited Walt Disney World before they had known each other, and you could say that it was a match perfectly made when these two people met and married many years later. He was a Disney fanatic, and she liked Disney too. Their love for Disney was evident quite early in their relationship from their respective Disney collections of Christmas tree ornaments and Disney movies.

You can just imagine their surprise and delight on their first Christmas together discovering what ornaments each of them had brought with them. Joe had collected the Disney glass Christmas balls, while Cheryl was a collector of the Disney figurines. In fact, 95% of their tree decorations are Disney from the Minnie Mouse angel tree topper, all the way down to the tree skirt at the bottom.

When the two had met nearly two decades before, Cheryl had a 4-year-old son, while Joe, who had been previously married, had no children of his own yet. The fact that they both loved Disney was a wonderful coincidence. "It was amazing how God had put us together. It was definitely magical meeting my wife and discovering our joint love for Disney," Joe said.

Each also had an extensive Disney movie collection. Much to their surprise, not one of them was a duplicate, "which was odd because there is so much Disney," Cheryl said.

Joe took Cheryl and her son to visit Walt Disney World not too long after that.

Just how important it was for these two people to be together was yet to come. In March 2015, Joe received a Stage 4 throat cancer diagnosis. This was particularly difficult as he had had a long career as a chef. Joe began his aggressive and gruelling 9-week chemo and radiation treatments. For the first two weeks, he did okay. But by the third week, he was starting to give up; even the Disney trip that had been meticulously planned by Cheryl and their travel agents couldn't keep Joe's spirits up. They had booked the vacation to celebrate finishing his treatments and to give him something to look forward to.

By then, the Biazzos had four children including a newborn they had just adopted, two full-time jobs and a joint part-time job on top of the cancer to deal with. For Cheryl to share that "it was a bit of a struggle" is an understatement if I've ever heard one.

Joe and Cheryl had always taken care of everybody else in their time of need, but the people that they had thought were their friends, even the people from the church they had gone to for three years, were not around for them. They appeared to have disappeared when things got rough. So they turned instead to their children's Christian school and thankfully, eight different pastors came to their assistance. "And some meals started coming in," Cheryl said. Unfortunately, though, Joe continued to go downhill and Cheryl could see it in his eyes.

In desperation, Cheryl turned to the folks in the Disney Facebook groups that she was a part of. Although these people were all strangers, their mutual love for Disney was about to become extraordinarily magical.

She posted to the groups what her husband and her family were going through. She asked if anyone might be able to drop Joe a card to cheer him up. It would be greatly appreciated. Cheryl thought that she would perhaps get a few responses. Cheryl also mentioned that Figment was Joe's favourite character. Since Joe was more "old school and not into email," Cheryl asked if she could get a few people to send a postcard; "something little like that so that every day he would get a reminder that people cared about him."

And with a little help from their friends – their Disney friends, that is what happened.

Messages began pouring in. And so did the gifts. Over 200 items were sent from all over the United States, Canada, the United Kingdom, Africa and even from the Disney cruise ships. The response was overwhelming; they couldn't believe all the cards and gifts that started arriving.

One of the first things that arrived was from a travel agent. It was a little game and photo frame from the Disney Cruise Line. A cruise line photographer sent a photo of Mickey and Minnie in their Christmas outfits and had it blown up for Joe. Another photographer from the UK sent photos as well.

Joe got a special Figment shirt available to pass-holders only during the Flower and Garden festival from Donna Jo, whose story "Disneyized" is in the first Positively Disney book. Joe and Cheryl are now dear friends with Donna Jo and her husband Billy, and see them whenever they visit Florida.

Joe received a pillowcase signed by all of the characters from cast members on a cruise ship. One of the hardest signatures to get is that of the Beast, and amazingly, that is on the pillowcase too. He took that pillowcase, along with the pillow his son had made for him, whenever he was hospitalized.

There were stuffed animals, a "humongous" purple Figment coffee mug, several pins, and even a Figment magic band from their travel agent friends who helped plan their upcoming trip. The item had sold out and was only available to cast members. When Joe saw that, he nearly cried; it meant so much to him. Cheryl regularly bought things for him as well to ensure that he would have a little Disney surprise every day.

Joe remembers the turning point of his fight. He was in the hospital for the second time and his sisters arrived from New Jersey. He realized that the determination of his wife, the love from his family, and the kindness and thoughtfulness of the Disney family; the culmination of them and God Himself were all there to help him beat his cancer. "One day I told myself *I'm not ready to check out*. I want to see my kids grow up. If I've got people fighting for me, then I've got to fight for me as well."

The Disney people were an inspiration for Joe to keep going. Of the cards and gifts he received, 80% were from Disney folks and they gave Joe hope and lifted his spirits. He could finally see the light at the end of the tunnel, he said. Joe completed his treatments in July 2016.

In October of that year, the Biazzos set off on their long-anticipated trip to Walt Disney World, celebrating life and celebrating Joe being cancer-free. Many cast members came up and congratulated him. Joe had also lost 60 pounds and was trying to rebuild his strength. So they just "took things in stride," Joe said.

It was wonderful. "We went to dinner, we got to meet characters. It was so enjoyable and refreshing. I'm so grateful and thankful," he said.

The Biazzos are truly grateful for the support they received from everyone, especially from their Disney family, most of whom they have never met. They decided that they wanted to give back somehow. And in that spirit of giving, they are buying Disney lanyards with pins in bulk, as many as they can.

Their kids give away a set number per day. That way, they too, can experience excited reactions from the recipients. They decided that they would either give a lanyard to a child who didn't have one or to a child who might not be having the best day. Not forgetting all the wonderful cast members, Cheryl makes little Ellie badges of grape soda caps to give something to them as well.

Disney folks are a special kind of people. Our love for Disney runs deep, and so do our connections with others who share this love, even if we haven't met them in person. The caring and compassion shown to this family was astounding. You never know how far a little pixie dust can go. It may even help save a person's life. It did in Joe's case.

A FRIENDSHIP FORGED

"We were really treated like royalty – every effort was made
by Disney to ensure that a great time was had by all."

— KIMBERLEY BOUCHARD

TWO THINGS THAT BRING ME great joy are Disney of course, and the Space Program. So when an opportunity – or more like an adventure – presented itself to spend a day at Walt Disney World with an astronaut, my husband and I were all over it. We were at a gala at Kennedy Space Center with a bunch of astronauts, crew, and other people while there for a shuttle launch. We were over the moon (pun intended)! To add to this glorious affair was a silent auction thus, the possibility of a day at Walt Disney World with an astronaut. Despite it being 2800 miles, or 4500 km from home for us, we were determined to do this. My husband and I watched the bidding stealthily. And as luck would have it, we won! We decided to return a few months later to redeem our prize. This was a win-win for us: we got to go to Walt Disney World and the recipients of the auction money were college students.

When I was thinking about the logistics of someone making themselves available to meet perfect strangers and spend a day at Walt Disney World with them, I thought it would be appropriate to properly introduce ourselves prior to meeting. Our three kids and my husband and I sent Captain Winston Scott (retired) an email of introduction through the organization responsible for setting this up. To our delight, he responded with an email of his own. We couldn't wait.

The countdown started.

I remember that day well, even though it was over a decade ago. It was a really hot and sunny September day. We were all supposed to meet in front of, fittingly, Mission Space at Epcot at a designated time in the morning. Captain Winston Scott, our chaperone, and the Disney ambassadors were waiting there for us. When I saw that our astronaut was wearing a jumpsuit – a blue one that is worn for these types of occasions, I felt really bad for him. I was cooking in my shirt and skort, and I could only imagine how he must have been feeling. I had brought along Canadian/American flag pins (we are Canadian) to give to everyone there. It turned out to be a nice icebreaker, and so our day began.

That day we experienced not only the special treatment of being a VIP at Walt Disney World, but we formed a special friendship with Winston and, later, with his wife Marilyn.

Our first adventure started out behind the scenes of Mission Space where we met astronaut Mickey for a photo shoot. Also behind the scenes, we got to learn the operation of the Mission Space attraction. Our three children were about 6, 8 and 10 years old at the time, which was perfect. So far so good!

I don't know what I was thinking; maybe I was just caught up in the excitement of everything, but "we" chose to ride the orange version of the attraction. For someone who gets dizzy on the Dumbo and Tea cup ride, I had no idea what I was in for. If I was out of my mind going on, you who have taken the orange version can imagine how I felt coming off. I excitedly jumped in with the astronaut and at least one of my sons (this part is a blur). And then it hit me. All of a sudden, I experienced the G force and spinning and I thought I was going to lose it. Oh, was I sick! Oh, was I dizzy by the end of the ride! It took everything in my power to not throw up. By that time I had no shame and no pride left. I took a complimentary barf bag supplied in the ride itself. (I still feel queasy just thinking about it!) I remained cool and casual and refused to upchuck in my "gift" bag. However, our daughter and I passed on the next ride, Space Mountain at Magic Kingdom. The photo we saw of my husband, two sons, and Winston at the end of that ride said it all. Hands all raised and grins a mile wide, they had really enjoyed that ride.

Reminiscing about this day recently, Winston still remembers that I grabbed the bag when leaving, but he was too polite to mention anything about it. He still is.

The rest of the day went by fantastically, although a bit blearily for me as I was still trying to get my head on straight. After a couple of hours though, I was pretty much back to form again.

A Disney ambassador drove us back to Epcot. I must say, we were treated like royalty. Every effort was made by Disney to ensure that a great time was had by all. We were never told an itinerary except when it came to meals. We could go on any ride at any time whenever we wanted! The Disney team kept the surprises and fun coming all day long.

While navigating the parks that day, we had a lot of time to get to know each other. We were really enjoying each other's company and discovered we shared a lot of the same family values. In addition, Winston and I discovered that we both played the trumpet. I don't play anymore, but Winston is a professional jazz musician. We have had the good fortune to hear him play, and our children have developed a fondness for jazz because of this.

Periodically we were stopped by people to ask if Winston was a real astronaut. His affirmative response brought cameras out and requests for photos. He was always gracious in complying but it started to get a little crazy. This is where the chaperone and ambassador came in; they would quickly usher us all through politely so we didn't end up spending a lot of time with other people requesting time with us.

Our final destination was dinner at the Coral Reef restaurant at Epcot. We were early, but we didn't mind. The conversation just kept flowing. Finally, our table became available and we followed a cast member in to be seated. Suddenly we stopped in our tracks. The table was not ready as we had been told, and our party of 7 was creating a bottle neck for patrons leaving the restaurant. With Winston in his jumpsuit, they wanted us to "disappear" rather quickly. So, into the butler's pantry we went. And *that* did it. This area was designed to house two, or perhaps three cast members running in and out quickly; we were a party of seven with two men over 6 feet tall! We all burst out laughing at the hilarity of our situation. I'm sure all the dinner guests walking by were wondering what we were all doing in that pantry laughing our heads off!

We were finally seated in two booths next to each other. My good-natured husband let me sit with Winston, our chaperone and our daughter, while he sat with our two sons (who have always been very well behaved at any restaurant or function, I may add).

As a left-handed person, I tend to have user issues with knives, especially when it comes to cutting anything I am about to eat. For whatever reason, I decided to order the pork chop off the menu. And there is where my troubles began. No matter how delicately I tried to cut up my food, it wasn't working. I sawed and ripped to no avail. To my dismay, I could not get my pork chop prepared to consume. I was breaking a sweat from trying and I was so embarrassed. Seeing my dilemma, Winston kindly offered to cut up my pork chop for me. He had it in bite-size pieces in no time. My embarrassment subsided and the humour of the situation bubbled over in laughter again. While he was cutting *all* of my dinner up for me so that I could eat it, I managed to get a photo. I sent a copy to Winston and signed it in the black marker typically used to sign photographs with the caption, "It's been a slice," and I signed my name. I have a similar one, minus the writing, hanging on our wall.

During dinner, I noticed the lovely salt and pepper shakers on the table and pointed them out to Winston and said I have a collection. The look on his face however, indicated that he thought I was going to pilfer them or something. When I realized what he was thinking, I nearly died. I told him quickly that I didn't steal the ones I have; I *bought* them from all over the world. He looked relieved at this and we had a good laugh over that one!

We were all so engrossed in our conversation that we lost track of the time. Our littlest guy for some reason, noticed the time on his new watch and alerted us. It was 8:45 and time to say good bye to Winston and run to the special dessert party for illuminations that our family was to attend. Perhaps it was the impending dessert party that had my son on full alert, I do not know. But this was the fastest goodbye we have ever said. It was sad that our day had come to an end, but we knew that we were going to be staying in touch.

To move from the restaurant saying our good byes, to the other side of the park in time for dessert and Illuminations within 15 minutes was daunting. We scrambled to find the special VIP area as the lights went down. We finally found it, and we sat down quickly to enjoy the show. We looked longingly at the desserts but the family passed on them. We found out later that the chaperone took Winston and got them a bit turned around. They never made it out of the park until the lights came back on. Winston said later that they should have just come along with us to see Illuminations too. I agreed.

Over the decade since, we have enjoyed meeting up with Winston and his wife whenever we are in Florida. We chat regularly on the phone, and they have been able to see the kids grow up. Who was to know that on one hot sunny day in front of Mission Space, a lifelong friendship would begin, a friendship forged most unexpectedly through circumstances and funny moments spent at the most magical place on earth, Walt Disney World.

DOUBLE ACTS OF KINDNESS

*"Making people happy and trying to bring out the good
in people is something I just do. It's about giving back
and making sure you can spread happiness and love."*

— MIKE ZEVON

THE FIRST TIME THAT MIKE visited Walt Disney World with his
wife Stephanie and his 5-year-old daughter Ellie, he was tak-
en aback. He had been on a bit of a disastrous trip with some
friends years earlier, but when he observed the reactions of
his family walking through the tunnel to Main Street USA
and seeing the castle for the first time, even he reacted. "I
just started to feel like wow – this place really is magical!"
This was only the beginning for the Zevon family. They experienced some magic that day while they were returning to
their resort that they in turn would spread themselves, in the
many years to come.

If you've been to Walt Disney World in August, you know that it tends to get very hot. And this day was no exception. It was beautiful, sunny, and "brutally" hot for the family. It was particularly hard on their little girl so they decided to head back to their resort where they could cool off and relax. They were grateful when the air-conditioned bus arrived to take them back.

While they were sitting there, they noticed the two other passengers sitting next to them: two young men in their early 20's were aboard with them. One was eagerly opening a box containing a new vinylmation to add to his collection. When he looked in the box, it appeared to Mike that he was disappointed with the figurine he got. As you do not know which one you get until you purchase and open the box, I can see why he might have been disappointed. It was Duffy the bear.

When Ellie saw it, her face lit up and she let out an audible "Oh wow!" The family didn't yet know what vinylmations were at the time. The young man saw her reaction and without missing a beat, he handed it to Ellie and told her, "Here, you can have it. I have doubles of this one."

Ellie was so excited and thanked the man. Mike and Stephanie were shocked that their daughter had spoken because she was so shy and introverted that she *never* spoke to anyone that she didn't know. "Seeing the reaction Ellie had opened my eyes to the magic of Disney," Mike said.

When the Zevons got back to their resort, they noticed that the resort also carried these vinylmations, so they decided to purchase a few. The Sleeping Beauty collection had just come out, Mike recalled.

When they discovered that they were getting some doubles of their own in their new collection, Ellie piped up, "Let's give *our* doubles away."

"That's what started it," said Mike. "It was pretty cool." "It" being their practice of vinylmation giveaways, also known as *double acts of kindness.*

Mike laughed when he told me about their collection. They have at least 500 of them now, and crazily enough, he got addicted to them. They have plenty of doubles to give away to others while they are visiting the parks. Whenever they are at Disney, the family bring their doubles along with them and while walking around the parks, they pick kids at random to give them to. The Zevons try to bring a variety of vinylmations with them and it is their daughter Ellie who asks the parents' permission to give one to their child/ children.

There are many vinylmations characters that include the classic Disney characters, Marvel Superheroes or Star Wars characters that the family brings along. The Zevons try to match the vinylmation to the child. "If we see a young man wearing a Star Wars shirt, then we'll try to give him a Kylo Ren double that we have. Or if someone is wearing a princess shirt, we'll give them one from the princess line," said Mike.

Their first giveaway took place in, appropriately, the Magic Kingdom. Ellie was told to look for children wearing superhero shirts. After spotting two, she asked the parents if it would be okay to give each of the children one. The parents were thrilled and said yes. The look on the children's faces reminded Mike of Ellie's face that day on the Disney bus when the young man was kind enough to give away his double to her.

On their trip in the summer of 2016, the Zevons were on the bus travelling from Disney Springs to the Whispering Canyon restaurant for their dinner reservation at Disney's Wilderness Lodge. Mike remembers that day well. It was pouring rain out and they boarded the bus quickly with another couple that had two daughters. They happened to have five or six vinylmations with them that day. They noticed that the girls were both celebrating birthdays, and Ellie gave them each a birthday vinylmation from the princess collection. "The look on their faces – they were thrilled. They were just so happy."

On another occasion after getting off the Haunted Mansion ride, the Zevons wandered into the store next door. A young boy walking through the store was wearing an Avengers shirt. Mike happened to have both a Black Panther and Captain America vinylmation with him, and he gave them both to the boy after checking with his mom to make sure it was alright to do so. The young man just stood there (probably in shock) and didn't know what to do. The mom thanked them and asked her son to do the same. He was still quietly standing there when suddenly the boy came right at Mike and hugged him. "I was like – wow!" That was really nice, just seeing their faces Mike says.

Once on a park day at Hollywood Studios, they encountered two brothers with toy light sabers. The Zevons gave them a Kylo Ren and Chewbacca vinylmation, making two little boys' and their parents' day a little extra magical.

While visiting Epcot, the Zevons had acquired doubles from the new Beauty and the Beast set. They found three different children that day to give them away to in yet more acts of kindness.

On another occasion, the family found themselves at Liberty Square in the Magic Kingdom by the rocking chairs. Mike had wanted to take a photo and noticed there was a father and son sitting there. He asked them if they would mind if he could just take a quick photograph. The son was very polite and moved out of the rocking chair right away for Mike. Mike wanted to give the boy an Iron Man vinylmation in appreciation for this courtesy. The father said it wasn't necessary, and they did not want to take it. Mike left it on the floor in front of the little boy and said, "that is yours," and walked away. The little boy picked it up and they finally accepted it.

That trip, the Zevon family gave away 33 vinylmations to children and incredibly, they have given away a 100 of them in total!

Mike said it makes his Disney experience better and at the same time teaches his daughter a valuable lesson. "Making people happy and trying to bring out the good in people is something I just do."

Ellie has a giving heart like her parents. She always wants to give out the vinylmations to other children they find. She has a big smile on her face when she does, because she knows she has just made someone else happy. "It's about giving back and making sure you can spread happiness and love."

The Zevons love Disney and now spend about two weeks at Walt Disney World each year. They are character hunters and especially like to see some of their favourites. Mike's are the stepsisters, Ellie's are Dopey and Arial, and Stephanie's is Belle. But what this family particularly loves is to spread extra magic for unsuspecting children at the parks.

These acts of kindness of giving a vinylmation double away causes a ripple effect. "You make the child's day and the parents' day and then they're going to tell people what happened and of course then it makes your day too," Mike said.

And that is what giving is all about really, isn't it?

MARATHON MAN

"It's where dreams come true and I'm going to do what I can do. And it's okay. I just have to try. It's okay for me if I can finish or not. It's Disney."

— GEOFFREY KANNER

AS SOMEONE WHO HAS FAILED miserably at the whole runDisney thing, I have found new inspiration in Geoff's story. I have previously signed up not once but twice for half-marathons including a back-to-back 10K and half-marathon, never to have them come to fruition. After speaking with Geoff, I have come to realize that I need to take baby steps. I need to be able to run a 5K before a 10K, and a 10K before a half-marathon. I recently got back on the treadmill on three occasions, and each time I go a little further. It's the little accomplishments that matter – like just even getting to the gym – that will make a difference and get me to where I want to be. I want to run a 10K. And then I want to run a half-marathon. I want to experience runDisney events. Sound like an impossibility for a gal with three college-age kids? Sometimes it does when I'm sore. But I digress. This is about Geoff Kanner and his journey.

A few short years ago, Geoff was an overweight middle-aged man with high blood pressure, high cholesterol, and diabetes and he was on medication to "fix" his ailments. He had gone for a stress test and failed it. The doctor cautioned him to be careful with any exercise program and told him specifically "don't run any marathons." Since that time, Geoff has become a multi-marathoner who is now off all medication and whose only ailments are temporary muscle strains due to his running adventures.

When Geoff's eldest daughter was a year old, his father passed away at an early age. Geoff told himself at the time that he didn't want to do something that would rob his kids the way he felt robbed from having a dad, and his kids from having their grandfather.

Still, life has a way of getting in the way. And Geoff became more out of shape as the years went by. When his daughter Stacey was a senior at university, she had been running races for awhile and both her parents were often there cheering her on from the sidelines. After a race, it was she that told her dad, "We've got to get you in shape. You've got to start running with me."

Geoff replied, "Oh, I don't know, Stacey. I don't think I can."

"Of course you can! You can do *anything*, but you've got to *want* to do it. And I *know* you want to do it," Stacey said. And she was right.

Geoff decided to do it. He started running around his neighbourhood. At first, he ran anywhere from 100-200 feet and then walked. The next day he did the same thing. On the third day, he added 50 feet. On the fourth day, he added another 50 feet. He would then add another 50 feet onto that. Then he would add a quarter mile.

And *little by little,* he eventually got to running and walking three miles. "After a few weeks, you find that you can run three miles. People don't think it can happen, but it can happen. It's really that simple."

When Geoff got to three miles, he added another quarter mile. "Some days I would ask myself – okay – how many *steps* is that? It's 1000 steps. Well 1000 steps – I can do that!"

Some days were tougher than others. "It's small steps, a little bit at a time. Break it up and it works."

It was January 2015 when he started eating healthier food and he began running. "I had this ache and that ache and this pain and that pain as anyone in their 50's does." But he continued anyway.

His first 5K was in April 2015. He barely got through it. He ran a little bit and walked a little bit, ran a little bit and walked a little bit. He finished it in 36 minutes, which was a pretty good time. However, he felt that he had failed because he had to walk part of it. After three months, he couldn't run three miles straight yet. Geoff got down to business and increased his training time to 4-5 times a week to prepare for a 10K he wanted to do. By June, he was running an incredible 4-5 miles nonstop. And *little by little*, he got stronger.

By October 2015, Geoff was signed up for his first half-marathon. He completed it in about 2 hours and 20 minutes. "I was thrilled with it." Before he had done his first half-marathon, all the training books had said that if you can train and do up to 10 miles, you can do a half-marathon. "And of course, like everybody else running their first half, I said no, no, I've got to run 15 miles to prove that I can run 13." When Geoff got to the starting line for his first half-marathon, he knew the distance was not going to be an issue because he had already run 15 miles to prepare.

"I learned something very powerful; there's really not anything I can't do if I set my mind to it. If another human being can do something (within reason), then I can do it also," Geoff shares.

Geoff continued running and signing up for local races. By the end of 2016, he had logged an incredible 1200 miles. It seems like a daunting amount, he said, and it would have been a year before, but breaking it up into small chunks made it possible for him to attain that. Sometimes it's still tough to get out, he said, but he feels mentally and physically great when he does. At about 500 yards in, he gets a smile on his face.

And Geoff's smile was about to grow bigger.

He and his daughter Stacey had just signed up for the Dopey challenge at Walt Disney World in 2017. The challenge involves four different races on four different days: a 5K, 10K, half- marathon, and a full marathon on the fourth day. A total of 48 miles in just four days!

They decided to go and just have a good time. Geoff wasn't doing the challenge for running a personal record. They were running for the experience. After all, how often do you get to do something like this? At the time, they thought that it would be a once-in-a-lifetime thing he shares.

Geoff is a big Disney fan. He has visited Walt Disney World close to twenty times. Missing an opportunity to go in high school, he first visited the park while he was a freshman in college. "It's a wonderful thing – being there with my in-laws and my family; it evokes a lot of memories."

To prepare for the Dopey challenge, Geoff found a trainer at his gym. As it turned out, he had known him in high school. He was a couple of years older than Geoff and in great shape. He knew and understood "older" bodies. "That's been terrific; that's been wonderful," Geoff shares.

He continued running other races, getting stronger and preparing himself for the Dopey Challenge, his biggest challenge to date.

By the time the Dopey Challenge was upon him, Geoff had been training for it by running four days in a row: 3 miles, 5 miles, 10 miles, then 19 miles.

Prior to registering for the race, he had looked up charities linked to the race on the runDisney website in case they couldn't get into the race. There are a limited number of spots available, but often if the race is sold out, you can run and raise money for various charities. As it turned out, he and Stacey registered successfully, but Geoff still wanted to help raise money at the same time. Being an air force veteran, Geoff chose the charity called Homes For Our Troops that builds mortgage-free homes for veterans that are disabled. "It's a phenomenal organization; 90% of the money raised actually goes to help the veterans." The minimum required to raise was just $600.

By reaching out to people and through Facebook, he experienced an outpouring of money. People would pledge $25 or $50, or whatever they wanted on a fundraising page that was set up for him. "It was quick and overwhelming. It was nice to see people support me for this." All of a sudden it wasn't just about doing this only for himself. "I'm representing a charity; I'm representing veterans and that kept me motivated."

And *little by little*, the pledges grew.

Geoff ended up being the number-one fundraiser for the charity. He singlehandedly raised over $3000 for it. "I thought that was pretty cool," he says.

The charity was happy that Geoff had signed up even though he was already registered for the race. This way, he could raise money to help the charity, and leave a spot available to someone else to run in one of the slots that the charity had available. Homes For Our Troops had approximately 100 people running in the four different races that weekend, Geoff said.

The race days arrived. Geoff and Stacey had to get up at 2:30 a.m. to get on the bus at around 3:30. "I needed a little coffee to get going," Geoff chuckled.

The entire 5K was done in the dark. The 10K was mostly done in the dark too, with the sun rising a little before they had finished. Running in the dark was a new experience for him as he hadn't trained for that. "But when you're at Disney, they have it well-lit so there was no problem seeing where we were going," he shares.

Finding out that the half-marathon had been cancelled because of the weather on the third day of the event was very disappointing. But what happened next was simply amazing. Thousands of runners went out running all around their respective resorts. Geoff and Stacey were at the Coronado Springs resort and they ran around the one mile-loop 13 times.

There were people cheering, and there was even a fellow in his 50's wearing a Peter Pan costume Geoff laughs, so he stopped for a character photo. Another group had a water station set up for them, and cast members came out to cheer the runners on and help hand out water. "That experience of running the *unofficial* half marathon was incredible. *That* was the real Disney spirit."

As much as he and everyone else would liked to have run the official half-marathon, "just having a couple dozen people cheering you on – that was pretty amazing – that was Disney at its best." And he, like everyone else who participated in the half that day, accepted their medals with pride.

They had earned it. The medals are not distributed for placement; they are distributed for completion at a pace set for no more than a 16-minute mile or faster, which Geoff and Stacey more than achieved. If anyone deserved that medal, it was Geoff. He had earned it long before, putting in many, many, many miles. He had committed to changing his lifestyle and he had successfully done so to accomplish this.

The runDisney races are for people who are unsure of their running ability. "I know I certainly was," Geoff says.

The biggest challenge that a lot of people have, Geoff said, is thinking that they *can't* do it. Thinking that way becomes defeating right from the very beginning. "Disney is the place that you *can* go and *finish* in the allotted 16-minute mile. Disney is safe; it allows people to get out there and say I'm going to try it." RunDisney has a special way of doing their events that Geoff believes no one else can replicate.

There were marching bands, choirs, characters, and singers all along the route. The volunteers were amazing too. The cast members were out there helping and happy to do so, even at 3 in the morning!

At the finish of the marathon every year, there is a gospel choir. "I don't know how long they stand out and sing for. When we finished at the 5½ hour mark, they were out there singing. And boy was that uplifting," Geoff shares.

"When a person crosses that finish line, everybody is cheering whether you are the last person or the first person." Geoff couldn't imagine the people ahead of him being treated better than what he was. "The cheering was tremendous. In fact, *everything* was. It didn't matter where you placed."

And *little by little*, Geoff changed.

He became healthy again; he ran and became a multi-marathoner completing 48 miles in a 4-day race. He became a *marathon man.*

"It's where dreams come true and I'm going to do what I can do. And it's okay I just have to try. It's okay for me if I can finish or not. It's Disney."

He and his daughter Stacey plan on signing up for both the Dopey challenge in 2018 and the Castaway challenge.

And *little by little,* dreams can come true.

MY GOOFY

"That was the best thing that could
have happened the whole trip."

—LISA MATTERS

ANY CAST MEMBERS I HAVE interviewed have shared similar mindsets when they tell me that they never know who they will meet, why a guest is at Disney, and what their back story might be. They have learned time and again that people visit Disney for all kinds of reasons. I would suspect also, that the characters have had just as powerful an experience meeting their guests as the guests do in meeting a character.

Lisa Matters has always liked Disney. "We owned every movie on VHS of Disney, I'm sure." When she told me that her favourite character was Goofy, I had to smile. I have not had too many women identify with him and I had to ask her why. She chuckled when she told me "I've always loved Goofy as a character because I'm a little goofy myself."

When Lisa began dating her husband, she noticed that he had a plush Goofy. To their delight, they discovered that they both had an affinity towards the fellow. Their mutual love for Goofy proved to be a good match. Keith would laugh like Goofy, act like Goofy and would often repeat Goofy's trademark quips. Lisa found it endearing and Keith was fond of Lisa's goofy side too. When Lisa married Keith, she knew that she was getting the package deal. Keith came with Goofy and goofy came with Keith.

Their family trip to Disneyland in July 1999 was a memorable one. Their son Jeremiah was 6, soon turning 7 years old while their daughter McKenzie, was 5 years old. They met a lot of characters that trip, and of course Goofy was on the roster to meet for these Goofy-loving parents.

Sadly, it was the family's first and final trip to Disneyland together for Keith tragically passed away that August.

Lisa raised her children with a strength she found through her faith. The little plush Goofy was a constant comfort and reminder of her husband and the love he shared with Lisa and his family.

Their son grew up and moved to California to study and he ended up working at Disneyland through the college program. He has a close bond with his mom, making sure that she is always okay. On Thanksgiving weekend in 2015, Lisa had the opportunity to visit him in California. They had planned on visiting a park and ended up at Disney's California

Adventure. Jeremiah wanted to show his mom around the park. The attractions and character meets were not a priority for them on that busy weekend. They didn't have a lot of time and were just happy to be able to spend it together.

Suddenly, Jeremiah turned to his mom and said, "You are never going to believe who I just saw."

Lisa knew that it could only be Goofy by the tone of Jeremiah's voice. The sighting was unexpected because it was a very unusual place and time for Goofy to be out.

The line to see him was amazingly short. Lisa wasn't sure how it would affect her to see Goofy face to face again, because the only time she had met him was with her husband, Keith. "My heart was already racing because we weren't expecting to see him."

When Lisa reached Goofy, she was trying to fight the tears that were threatening to come to the surface. The photographer was taking a lot of photos and she was trying everything she could to hold her emotions in check. She held on to Goofy's hand and she began to cry. When she held his hand, it was the tightest grip ever, she said. "You could tell that I was hanging on for dear life in the photo because the muscles in my forearm were popping out," she shared. *I'm not letting you go* Lisa thought. It was her connection to her husband, *her* Goofy.

I can only imagine the grip she had on him as Lisa is a registered massage therapist with very strong hands.

Lisa was grateful that the photographer had caught her joyful expression before tears began to flood her face. A moment later, she hugged Goofy and all the tears over the loss of *her* Goofy came to the surface.

And Goofy held on.

Jeremiah walked over and quietly told Goofy, "You'll never know what you mean to my mom." He was very emotional too, because he knew just how much Goofy *had* meant to his mom.

Lisa wanted to say something but it wasn't possible. There was no way that she was going to get two words out. She wished that Goofy could have spoken to her.

After her encounter, Jeremiah told his mom that he was close to tears as well because he had seen how excited and happy she had been to see Goofy. "That was the best thing that could have happened on the whole trip," Lisa said.

The little plush Goofy now has a place of its own on a chair in Lisa's room. Very few people are allowed to sit in the chair, let alone handle Goofy.

A recent gift Lisa received at Christmas in 2016 was from Jeremiah. By the look on his face when he gave her his gift, Lisa knew it had to be something to do with Goofy.

And she was right. It was a beautiful clay sculpture of Goofy. She hugged her son and couldn't stop crying. Jeremiah had known how happy his mom would be to receive this special gift.

Lisa will always have a special place in her heart for Goofy. She will never forget the unexpected encounter with him on that Thanksgiving weekend with her son. They were in the right place at just the right time.

"Everybody was probably wondering what's my story? when I met Goofy that day," said Lisa

And now you know.

THE ART OF LIFE

"I certainly have always been influenced
by Walt – the businessman."

—*Disney Master Artist Kevin-John Jobczynski*

For as long as he could remember, Kevin-John always wanted to replicate the things he enjoyed on paper with his pencils and crayons. Like many youngsters, he enjoyed Batman, dinosaurs, and Star Wars. Thus, these were the subjects of his first works of art. He has certainly come a long way as a Disney master artist since those early drawings, but everyone has to start somewhere!

Kevin-John's first experience at a Disney park was at Disneyland when he was 8 years old. His family had recently moved to California and lived there for two years. Kevin-John had seen some of the Disney movies, but there was a "strong emphasis on princesses so there was a little bit of a disconnect there for a little boy. I loved the live action stuff," he says.

Walking into Disneyland was something else entirely to little Kevin-John. "It was the most incredible thing I had ever seen. It was like walking into a storybook and being able to live within these worlds. For me, I still haven't shaken that wanderlust of a young child in many ways." He loved the Haunted Mansion and believed that the ghosts were real. He couldn't see any strings and tried to figure out how Walt got the ghosts to live there – quite a conundrum for a little boy to understand.

As Kevin-John got older, he continued drawing, honing his skills in black-and-white, pen-and-ink drawings. His strength was always in drawing with a lot of attention given to the detail within those drawings. Less than a decade later at just 17, Kevin-John had grown into quite a fine artist, and he began building his brand to what we now see today.

His early work as a professional artist in his hometown of Erie, Pennsylvania, dealt with local historical landmarks and buildings and points of interest. One subject of special interest he drew is the wooden hulled ship called the U.S Brig Niagara, a battleship that was constructed there and used in the Battle of Lake Erie.

After drawing every conceivable landmark and point of interest in his little town of Erie, PA, Kevin-John made the transition into sports art. Along with drawing, Kevin-John played and coached football. He enjoyed playing, coaching and watching sports a lot, so it was a natural transition for him. Because of his playing, he was "intimately familiar with how the body reacts and looks when playing a sport," which is essential if you are drawing action portraits.

And as in his childhood, he still loved to draw the things that he enjoyed.

The action portraiture he was drawing initially began when a football player commissioned Kevin John to create a portrait of him in action to be displayed in his new restaurant. Over the next 20 years, Kevin-John would gain national recognition for his sports art. He has since been commissioned to draw more than 350 pro-athletes and their teams, and continues to be commissioned today.

Although his incredible career has spanned over 30 years now, it has not been easy for Kevin-John. As a matter of fact, some of the obstacles he has faced and overcome would be enough for any other person to just throw in the towel. You see, Kevin-John is colour-blind. It is a disability that most people learn to live with, but is particularly debilitating for an artist.

He also lives with severe rheumatoid arthritis and was diagnosed with it at age 24. I can only imagine how painful painting could become for him. It snatched his athletic career, it snatched a lot of physical things he used to enjoy doing, and it almost snatched his career as an artist from him. He was not going to let his career as an artist be taken from him too. So he continued to work, and work hard despite the pain, despite his colour blindness, and despite not being encouraged to follow his art as a career. Kevin-John is not quick to share this with people because he wants people to buy his art for his art, and not buy it out of sympathy for him. I think we can all attest to the fact that we *love* his art and *that's* why we buy it.

Like so many successful artists who can make a living with their art, he was only encouraged to keep it as a hobby. And like many, he worked at a "regular job" at one point to make ends meet. In fact, Kevin-John was working 40 hours a week at his regular job and putting in another 30 to 40 hours a week on his art. He realized that he wouldn't have a career as an artist by working part time on it, so with a little faith, he eventually decided to take the plunge, despite being told differently. "If you don't want me to succeed, the worst thing you can tell me is that I can't do it. If you tell me I can't do something, then I'm going to spend the next 20 years proving you wrong," he says.

It was this mindset that helped him get through the rough times in his 20's. He believes that it's fear more than anything that keeps people from realizing their dreams. "You can't be scared when they are about to turn off your electricity or you have only two nickels left in your pocket and you're hungry. You cannot allow these things to scare you. Failure is a good thing. I think you learn so much from failing. The people that are able to get themselves up from the 'bloody' canvas one more time and stay in the fight and *learn* from that failure are the ones to succeed the most."

Without any artist role models in his life, Kevin-John looked to other people earning a living from their natural talents and abilities such as authors, musicians, athletes, and actors; all of those earning a living in a non-traditional career. Kevin-John wisely states that the talent will take care of itself. It's all the other components that will make you successful or not: understanding the market and **hard work.** "You run it as a business, not as an art. I realized that very early and that was my direction very early. I had an ability that the other kids in my class didn't necessarily have and I was always the best in my class." *But what was I going to do with that talent?* He asked of himself.

An inspiration for Kevin-John was actually Walt Disney. "I certainly have been influenced by Walt, the businessman... and the fact that he was an artist and found different ways to become employed." It was always his favourite part of the *Wonderful World of Disney, World of Color* show on television when Walt would appear and speak to the audience.

As Kevin-John continued his work as a sports portraiture artist, different opportunities would come his way. One of these opportunities was with ESPN doing artwork live at sporting events. However, there was a catch. Instead of the black-and-white compositions that Kevin-John drew, they wanted colour so that it would "pop out" on television making it better for all to see. Kevin-John had never worked in colour save for the very early years when he would draw and colour with his crayons. The fact that he was colour blind was not going to hold him back from this golden opportunity. "If I was going to fail, it wasn't going to be because of that." So, Kevin-John went home and taught himself how to paint. He would work 40-50 hours a week on his contracted work and another 20-30 hours a week learning how to paint. He humbly acknowledged that "now I paint at a world-class level, but back then I certainly wasn't."

Kevin-John explained that a lot of people don't understand about painting where there is colour within the colour. You don't just add black to make a shadow. Shadows are actually varying shades of purple or when painting folds or creases, you need to think about what colour does in order to replicate that, he says. "I don't have the ability to identify the colours within the colours, so I have to create it."

Listening to Kevin-John, I understand to a better degree now why we teach the science behind creating colours. This is so important. There is so much more to painting than I ever thought there was, and I used to paint in my younger days too!

Kevin-John by this time was a national prominence with his sports art. He had been working professionally for about 25 years when his work caught the eye of Disney.

At the time, his particular style with his sports figures was what is called "dripping torso." Since he wasn't featuring a background, his sports figures were finished off with paint literally running off the page. "This dripping took on a kind of character of its own, and Disney really liked it."

When Disney approached him, they were interested in having him duplicate the park experience in fine art such as replicating the audio animatronics featured in the park, in the attractions, and in the scenery. They wanted to give people the park experience to take home with them and hang on their walls. "That I understood, that I could do." And the rest they say, is history.

Kevin-John remembers visiting Walt Disney World for the first time in his late 20's. He will never forget it. "It was a life-changing experience – it was so much more than what I remember Disneyland being. You could escape from the world and you could enter these gates and the outside world just didn't invade." He also remembers the first time walking into one of the galleries there and looking at all the paintings hanging on the walls. He thought *no way in a million years would I be that good. Never could I see my art hanging in a place like that.* He didn't paint at the time and Kevin-John knew – or thought he knew – his limitations. I always say never say never, especially when it comes to Disney!

Ten years from that first visit, his art was featured in the very same galleries. "It's crazy," he laughed. "You don't always see the path that is laid out in front of you. Sometimes it's a matter of just trusting yourself to walk into the forest and find your way. And often, a path *will* present itself. You have to believe in yourself and believe in fate sometimes."

Kevin-John was enthused by what Disney was asking of him. What he likes most about Disney is the parks; the immersion experiences that one can have there. "And now I'm able to give that to people through my art work for them to bring home and hang on their walls."

His original pieces of art are typically purchased within hours and sometimes within minutes of being displayed to the public in the galleries. It is common for his paintings to be sold while they are still in the concept stage as well. "It's very cool, but it's crazy because for the most part, people don't get to always see (and enjoy) the original."

He finds the Disney community very warm and support-ive. "It's all love. I've never received a nasty email or mes-sage because I painted Figment instead of Mickey Mouse or I painted something from the Haunted Mansion instead of Snow White." The Disney fan base is very large and loyal and strong. And Kevin-John's work really resonates with them, becoming instantly popular with the fans. Kevin-John feels that it is a blessing that his Disney art is so well received. "Creating art for Walt's company is the biggest honour that has ever been bestowed upon me." And we in turn, are blessed because of it.

And this... is the *art* of life.

HAPPINESS BY CHANCE

*"To these guys, to these girls who don't have a lot
of friends, who have so much trouble with social
relationships, it's just amazing – the impact: physical,
cognitive, emotional, social that Disney has."*

—DIANE MYERS

ONCE UPON A TIME, THERE was a little boy named Chance. He came into this world at St. Joseph's Hospital, not far from the Walt Disney Studios in California. He did not know that he would grow up as a special gift to his mom and to all those that he encountered.

You see, he had special powers. Not in the way that you would see in a fictional super hero though. His powers were far more valuable than that. Chance's powers were exceptional because they were about happiness. He had the power to bring happiness to others, especially to those that were spreading happiness themselves.

Although he lived in a world that was sometimes cruel and mean, he learned through the kindness and gentleness shown by his mother that not all people are cruel; there is kindness in the world. His mom would show him a place where this was sure and true. She would tell her son, "You can never lose faith in people, honey. There are good people out there." She would remind him too, "that's why Disney is so special to us."

It was not always easy for Chance and his mom Diane, to be in the most magical place on earth. Like them, there were a whole lot of other people visiting there at the same time, excited to experience this wonderful place also. Being on the autism spectrum, Chance had his challenges at Disney. The sensory overload we experience can be intense and sometimes we even need a break from it. For a person who is autistic, this is intensified and can be difficult to cope with at times.

Diane recalled the time when Chance was about 10 years old and they were standing in line for the Winnie the Pooh ride. For reasons unknown to her, Chance had an "epic meltdown" that left them no other choice but to leave the line and leave the park. "It's a good thing I like to hang out at the resorts," Diane chuckles. No matter what their plans were, sometimes Chance just couldn't handle it anymore. Sometimes it would be just too much wonderful.

On another occasion, when they were about to enter the Haunted Mansion, they had to suddenly turn away and pass up on the ride. Chance had just had enough. Numerous times they would have to leave the park early and go back to the quiet of their resort.

Throughout the years, however, things improved. They would be able to ride the attractions without incident. One day when Chance was 16 years of age, they were in line to ride the Haunted Mansion once again. Suddenly, he turned to his mom and told her that he would like to ride it all by himself. Diane was stunned. Chance had to have summoned up everything that he had to tell her this, Diane shares.

They eventually found out about the Disability Access Pass, now called the Disability Access Service or DAS card. It is designed to make it easier for people with disabilities, whether "seen or unseen," to access the attractions. After a change in policy regarding the cards, Diane thought it would be a good idea to engage cast members in a conversation to help facilitate some understanding about autism, an often "unseen" disability.

To achieve this, Diane thought it would be good for Chance to ask cast members for their autograph. The autograph book started out very small with just a few cast member autographs on that trip. Chance was learning to approach others and engage them in conversation. It was so important for him to feel comfortable enough to approach them. "A lot of autistic kids just don't engage people, and it's one of the most difficult things to do." Chance knows that Disney is his safe place, Diane said.

Prior to their visit in October 2016, Diane posted on a popular Disney Facebook page with cast members and told them about the autograph project. She explained that Chance was autistic and that he collected autographs from cast members. This caught the eye of several Facebook members as did the t-shirts and the buttons for his lanyard that Diane had made that said "I [heart] Cast members."

"You wouldn't believe the number of cast members who approached Chance when they saw his shirt and buttons."

"That's so cool!" and "Thank you so much!" were said again and again with an additional hug or handshake shared with them.

The cast members who saw the post messaged Diane that she and Chance could meet them in the park when they went to the Magic Kingdom for the Halloween party, which also coincided with Chance's birthday.

The first meetup was with a couple of cast members at the Emporium on Main Street USA. They were delighted to meet each other and signed Chance's book. They asked Diane and Chance to come back at 9:30 that evening. "We'll have something very special," they told them.

Upon returning to the Emporium, the two cast members had gathered all of the other cast members to stand around Chance where they proceeded to sing "Happy Birthday" to him. "Chance stood there just tickled," Diane shared.

At Star Traders, the cast member happily signed his autograph book and told Chance that he could pick out whatever he wanted. Even though Chance is 27 years old, he still likes stuffed animals. He picked one out and had his picture taken with the young lady.

On another occasion in Epcot, they were in Mouse Gears when he asked two cast members for their autographs. One called her mom immediately, she was so excited. "Mom, you're never going to believe this. Somebody has just asked *me* for an autograph!"

"I thought that they were going to faint and fall on the floor," Diane laughed.

At Raglan Road, the Irish pub and restaurant at Disney Springs, Chance had the band and Irish dancers signing his autograph book, and they had Chance go up on stage and take a photo with them. The band even dedicated a song to him. "It's been the most amazing place ever."

Chance had finally mastered his invitation to sign his autograph book. Where Diane at one time had to prompt Chance, he now does it all on his own. He has the whole thing down pat: "Hi my name is Chance, and I collect cast member autographs because I believe you bring the magic…" He would approach everybody from security to dining room staff, to the luggage guys and the cast members on the boat docks." The cast members are thrilled to be asked. "I cannot tell you how many times they'll look at him and say that he's the first person that ever asked them for their autograph." On that trip in October, Chance acquired 120 cast member autographs!

Sometimes Diane and Chance will meet up with people to go to Walt Disney World together; other times they will go solo. There are a variety of groups that Diane is a part of that can assist visitors who have family and friends with special needs. Some of these groups are Tips for Special Needs; Walt Disney World Made Easy for Everyone, and My DAS.

Diane works three jobs so that they can go to Walt Disney World every other year. Chance works as a pastoral assistant to do the little jobs that need done around their church once a week. He is also the backup maintenance man at their apartment building. Their dream is to move to Florida one day where Chance would like to work for Disney as a groundskeeper or as Pluto, Diane shares.

They have had many, many positive experiences with many, many understanding, aware, compassionate, and patient cast members. Diane has seen her son grow in confidence and courage with a spark in his eagerness to learn and explore. "Many of our kids, even our autistic adults, are so enamored with what Disney does and the magic of it. To these guys, to these girls who don't have a lot of friends, who have so much trouble in social relationships – it's just amazing the impact: physical, cognitive, emotional, social that Disney has."

And an amazing thing happened to this young man named Chance. The more happiness that he gave, the more it spread, and the more it was returned to him. Sharing what was sure and true. That this place, in this world of Disney, *was indeed* a kind and magical place.

SPECIAL AFFECTS

"Working at Disney made me a whole new
person that I absolutely love. I'm driven, and
I know what I want to do with my life."

— EMMALINE JOHNSON

LIKE ANYTHING NEW THAT WE encounter, we have expectations about it. We have preconceived notions of how it might turn out; be it a new job, a new home, a relationship, even a vacation. And isn't it wonderful when we can go to a place and have it meet all of our expectations and even more? This is exactly what happened to Emmaline Johnson, a student from the University of Mississippi, which is affectionally known as "Ole Miss," located in Oxford, Mississippi.

Emmaline has always loved Disney. She grew up in a family of Disney fans and says she's seen every single Disney movie. Her first visit to Walt Disney World took place when she was just 2 years old; her second visit was when she was 7. By the time she was 14 years old, in 2011, her family was visiting Walt Disney World every year. On a couple of occasions, Emmaline was there for a baton competition called Twirl Mania. It is an international championship competition for baton twirling, pompom, and dance contestants that encompasses everyone at every level and age from around the world. It includes world-class instruction and performances that take place at Walt Disney World annually. She was able to perform in a choreographed piece at Walt Disney World, but it wasn't experienced at a Disney park. Thus, her dream to be a baton twirler at Walt Disney World began.

Emmaline's mother had been a college twirler herself and she enrolled her daughter in lessons at the tender age of 5. Emmaline admitted to me that "I was the most uncoordinated person ever. I was probably the worst twirler ever." The instructors had even asked her mom if she would remove Emmaline from the class; she was that bad. Undaunted, Emmaline remained. It took her two years just to do a cart wheel, but her tenacity and hard work paid off. She became one of only three featured twirlers at her university, a very prestigious position Emmaline shares.

In 2015, Emmaline's parents met a young woman who had participated in the college program at Walt Disney World. Emmaline had known a few people who had gone through the program as well. After being contacted by the young woman and being encouraged to try it out, Emmaline applied. A few days later she found out that she was accepted into the program. She was excited but was a little unsure yet about leaving her university for a semester. She had just started dating her boyfriend and she was trying to finish her marketing program. However, excitement and anticipation won her over, and she moved to Florida.

When she arrived, she learned she'd been assigned to merchandising in Hollywood Studios, her favourite park. When Disney told her where she would work, she couldn't believe it. Without letting them know where she wanted to work, they had assigned her to the exact park, the exact street, and the exact store that she wanted to work at. She took it as a good sign and a great start.

When people found out that she was going to be a cast member, she was told that Disney would not be the same for her, that she might have the magic of her experiences as a returning guest ruined somehow.

"This is a fair assumption because of all the magic you will learn about that takes place behind the scenes." However, Emmaline would beg to differ. "I'll tell you, being a cast member, you gain this whole new love, this whole new appreciation because you see all of the stuff they have to do, and all the training that the cast members do. It was nice to experience it and learn everything."

Emmaline had many, many great experiences at Walt Disney World as a cast member. Once she met a lovely, sweet gentleman who was 85 years old and spoke with him for about 45 minutes. He was on a family trip with his son and granddaughter. He shared with Emmaline through his big grin that she had made his day. Emmaline assured the older gentlemen that it was in fact him, who had made *her* day. She loved that she could meet so many amazing people and not get reprimanded for speaking to guests like you would in another job. A little while later, the son and granddaughter came back to speak with Emmaline. They told her that she really had made the older man's day. He had just lost his wife the week before, and this was the first time that they had seen him enjoy himself in a very long time.

Emmaline was so touched that she had to ask for a break to compose herself. It hit her hard. "It broke my heart to hear this. I learned you never know what somebody is going through at Disney."

When a person goes to visit a Disney park, it's a privilege she says. As a cast member, Emmaline had underestimated the impact of Disney on its guests while she was enjoying it so much herself. But when she learned about the stories of *why* people were there and the affect Disney had on them, it was amazing. "The guests think that they are getting a life-changing experience, but as a cast member, we are getting just as much, if not more of a life-changing experience."

Another time a little girl was visiting the park with her dad and older sister who was 6 years of age. Her mom had recently passed away. The little girl had gone off to use the restroom and for some reason couldn't find her dad when she came out again. She was crying, and she was lost. The only person that the little girl would speak to was Emmaline. She spent an hour with the girl, trying to figure out how to get a hold of the dad as she did not know his number, and she had no identification on her. When the little girl settled down, she asked Emmaline if they could go get some ice cream. The little girl was reunited with her worried family a little while later. "You get to experience a lot of things and you realize just how blessed you really are in life."

Emmaline especially enjoyed the parks as a cast member. She could enjoy the parks herself every day after work. She even timed the most opportune times to get on her favourite rides: Splash Mountain and Rock N Roller Coaster Starring Aerosmith. She lost track of just how *many* times she rode the rides after she reached 100.

She also enjoyed it when people would come to visit her. "When my mom came, it was the coolest thing because I got to show her where I worked." Her boyfriend, who was studying in South Carolina, came regularly to visit Emmaline and experience Disney right along with her. For everyone who came to visit her, she was their professional "unpaid tour guide," she laughs.

Emmaline found out that her school's marching band which she had twirled baton in, was going to be at Walt Disney World on Labor Day weekend. Her college program would be coming to an end the last day of May. Knowing that she would be coming back to twirl in a Disney parade a few months later, made her remaining time at Walt Disney World extra-special. She would watch the parades and think *that is going to be me someday; that's going to be me in September.* "It's always been a lifelong dream of mine to be able to be a featured twirler wearing the prestigious costume that I've worked my whole life for, in front of the castle. It was like the cherry on the cake."

The day finally arrived. They had rehearsed back at home following the guidelines that Disney had set out for them. A few hours before the parade began, they rehearsed and got their approval for everything that they were planning on doing in the parade as twirlers. Although it started raining, that was not going to change how Emmaline was feeling. A lifelong passion that lead to her dream was about to happen.

The characters on foot were just behind them. Emmaline and the two other featured twirlers were the first ones out. The drum majors, the colour guard, and the marching band followed in that order. Immediately following the band was the Disney parade itself.

They moved a lot quicker than what they normally did in other parades. They had to be careful of the trolley tracks as well. They were so excited and had so much adrenaline that they matched the pace of the parade easily. The parade started at Splash Mountain, went through Frontierland, across the bridge around the circle in front of the castle, and finished at the end of Main Street USA.

It was an even bigger deal for Emmaline to be there that day. All of her fellow cast members she had worked with as well as family and friends were there to cheer her on. "I had a lot of people yelling my name and taking pictures" she said, smiling at the memory.

Working at Disney was a game changer for her. It affected her in so many different ways. When she went to the Disney college program, she had felt lost; she did not know what she wanted to do or know what kind of person she wanted to become. "Working at Disney made me a whole new person that I absolutely love; I'm driven, and I know what I want to do with my life."

"When you work at Disney, you get to learn all of these amazing skills that you just would never get working somewhere else." It gave her a whole new perspective on her life; it made her happier and it made her grow up a little. "I met some of the greatest people while I worked there, and I remember a lot of the older, full time cast members fondly. It's because of Disney that I started getting my life together; Disney brought me closer to my boyfriend; Disney brought me closer to my family."

Working at Walt Disney World and fulfilling a lifelong dream to twirl in a Disney parade affected Emmaline profoundly. It gave her the perspective of being a child once again. "You just get all of these new ideas – I feel like I've just restarted my childhood over again. I've got all of these different emotions and feelings again for all of these different things."

The affect that Disney has on us as guests, is extraordinary. But its affect on its cast members I believe, is even more so.

POWER PRINCESS

"We all have this power to make someone else happy
and it doesn't just have to be in a princess costume."

— KYLEE MCGRANE, COFOUNDER: A MOMENT OF MAGIC

THE YOUNG WOMAN YOU ARE about to meet was born with the heart of a princess and the strength of a warrior. Her strength and grace combined with her compassion, love, and caring for the sick children she meets are amazing.

As a youngster, Kylee McGrane was obsessed with Disney and wanted to be a Disney princess so much that she ruined many Disney VHS movies from rewinding them to watch over and over again. She loved to play make-believe and pretend to be a princess. "I was really inspired by the princesses and everything that they stood for." Visiting Walt Disney World a handful of times, she would drive her younger sisters crazy because she wanted to get pictures with all of the princesses before going on any rides.

During Christmas 2014 and while home in Pennsylvania on her break, Kylee's parents decided that they were going to have a family day and watch *Frozen* together. "You've got to watch this movie – you're going to love it!" Her parents told her. Little did Kylee know that she was about to discover what would turn into her life-calling.

While she was watching the movie, the wheels began turning in her head. Looking at Elsa, Kylee thought to herself *I kind of look like that – I have the blonde hair, blue eyes, and fair skin.* "There was something about that movie. We all connected with it, but it was the story of the sisterhood, the overall message, especially the phrase 'love is an open door' that struck a chord with me."

Along with being an avid Disney fan, Kylee is also Taylor Swift's biggest fan she claims. Ms. Swift does a lot of work in the pediatric cancer community and it had always inspired her to get involved, too. But Kylee had been afraid, unsure if she could emotionally handle it. During the movie, Kylee had what she calls an epiphany. "It was just the magical occurrence of all of these things, all of the things that I loved, culminating into one idea."

She texted her best friend Maggie and asked her what she thought about dressing up as Princesses Elsa and Anna and visiting pediatric hospitals. "Yes! Let's do it! Why not?" was her response. And the seed for A Moment of Magic foundation was planted.

Kylee and Maggie raised funds to purchase the costumes. It's expensive and they wanted professional grade costumes Kylee says. They wanted them to be as close as possible to the costumes depicted in the movie. "We take our character integrity really seriously," Kylee says.

The first road block was getting into the hospitals. As neither one of them had volunteer experience in hospitals, they needed to work their way up to that. There are a lot of things to know and various precautions to be taken, especially when dealing with children who are battling a life-threatening illness. Undaunted, the young women began with smaller events where they would visit special education schools. Armed with photos of themselves in action and recommendation letters, they had their first hospital visit in May 2015 at Cohen Children's Medical Center nearby. "That first hospital experience was so life-changing that we just fell in love with it."

They now visit pediatric hospitals and social services institutions, and they work with other non-profit organisations that work especially with pediatric cancer patients. Their company has 40 volunteers: 20 princesses and 20 magic makers. The magic makers are just as important and special as the princesses, and they are encouraged to interact with the children as well.

Hospital visits can range from playroom parties with crafts, reading books, and doing sing-alongs to individual bedside visits. These latter are their favourite. They love to spend one-on-one time with a child and make them feel important and special, all that these children deserve.

They never set an end time to their visits. They feel that "if pediatric cancer doesn't stop, then neither should we." Their visits can go from 1½ hours to 2 hour and on occasion, up to 6 hours at a time. They do a lot of walks for pediatric cancer which involve volunteers, families, fighters, and survivors. They all walk to raise money and awareness. This can get a bit gruelling at times because not only are the princesses in costume for the duration, they are also in character as well.

All princesses (and magic makers for a lesser extent) must undergo princess training, which includes 40 hours of volunteer work, shadowing a princess. Through their training, princesses work at dressing, posing, speaking, and singing like a princess. They also learn about HIPAA laws in the United States, interacting with children with special needs and terminal illnesses, what to talk about and what not to talk about. And they learn what to do in case of an emergency.

Kylee has been on over one hundred and fifty visits. She and Maggie have learned a lot about hospital standards from child specialists and other health care professionals. They bring this back to their princess training program and expand on it. Most importantly, they do not talk about a patient's illness or ask how they are doing; instead they ask who their favourite character is or what their favourite song is and why. "We want to take this child's experience, even if they're in a hospital room, and remove them from the hospital room mentally."

They meet little boys as well as little girls. "Don't let them fool you – the boys love princesses. They really do. We go in and they giggle and they ask about Olaf." The boys have sometimes been more excited than the girls to meet the princesses.

Kylee can't stress enough about how she feels every single time she goes out to visit these children. She has had so many incredible life-changing moments that make her light up. When she sees a child, who calls out to her as Elsa and sees their excitement and joy upon seeing her, it makes her feel "indescribably happy."

On one visit, a little girl was just turning 4 years old. She was going home for hospice care as there was nothing more that could be done for her. When Kylee walked into the room, she says she will never, ever forget the sound of the little girl's adorable high-pitched voice exclaiming "Elsa! It's You!" It was a magic moment that they were creating for this little one. Her last wish was to have a tea party with a princess. "Knowing that we were able to make her wish come true is just something that I'm so grateful for and that *this* opportunity through this organization came to me. It is just one of the most powerful feelings that you can make someone's dream come true. It gives me purpose in my life."

It is difficult and emotionally draining to see these children going through these terrible experiences and the fight for their lives. Support from her own family and friends and knowing that she has made a child happy gives Kylee some solace. They hold on to the idea that they have been *privileged* to celebrate the child's life and get to know him or her as a person to help get them through a heart wrenching visit.

The foundation recognizes that being a princess or magic maker is not for everybody because of its emotional impact on a person. However, there are many other ways people can help. Donating toys and gift cards and participating in walks to raise money and awareness are all helpful. The foundation donates prom dresses to the hospitals that hold proms. Anything they can find that can help make these children feel special is what they strive for. "We buy a lot of crowns" Kylee shares.

The foundation also does a "Wear Your Crown" presentation in high schools where the women speak about confidence, female empowerment, and finding your passion in service work. "It's about wearing your invisible crown every day and knowing to keep your head up or your crown is going to fall off."

Joining forces with her and Maggie on three hospital visits was Miss New York, Serena Bucha, who is a high school friend of Kylee's boyfriend. "It was really cool to work with someone that literally looks like a Disney princess in real life. The kindness and confidence she exuded while addressing the older children was incredible." Serena connected with a lot of the older kids whereas Kylee and Maggie connect with the younger ones. "It was really cool to encompass all of the things that we wanted to encompass in that visit. She was just incredible."

Kylee loves her job. In fact, she loves *everything* about it. But she hopes one day that she won't have to do it anymore because childhood cancer will have become eradicated. She is also an advocate on the pediatric cancer platform and continues to educate herself and others on the subject. "People are not aware of this horrible disease in children," she said. And she wants to change that.

In the meantime, Kylee is in her final year of university with a double major in English and Communication with a business minor. She devotes about 50 hours of her time each week to the foundation. Upon completing university, Kylee wants to work at the foundation full time and eventually head it up. The foundation is setting up college chapters and has developed a "ready to go" package for those that would like to be a part of this.

Kylee was inundated with over eight hundred emails two weeks after a video clip about the work they do went viral with 22 million views at the time. They are working hard to fulfill the needs of those requesting princess visits. "There is nothing more frustrating than receiving an email request from a mother across the country and not being able to be physically there." In the interim, Skype visits have been quite successful in reaching out to children across the country. They have connected with 5000 children in 17 states and 2 countries to date.

I am so grateful to be able to write and share about this foundation with others. What this foundation is doing is phenomenal. The kindness, compassion, and caring bestowed upon some of the sickest and most vulnerable in our world is admirable. "It's knowing that no matter how sick a child is or what they have gone through, or their treatment that day, we all have this power to make someone else happy and it doesn't just have to be in a princess costume.".

And this my friends, is what a Power Princess is.

If you would like more information on the foundation visit www.amomentofmagic.com.

TSUM TSUMS WITH HEART

*"It's been good fun and quite fulfilling because
you see how excited people are to get them."*

— *ABI FORREST*

I AM ALWAYS AMAZED TO hear about how something from one's childhood, influences them in their adulthood. And when it involves something Disney, I find it fascinating.

Abi's family were always huge Disney fans. Growing up in Scotland, Abi watched all the Disney films. On birthdays, her dad would take them to the cinema to see the newly released Disney movies. When Abi was 2 years old, her world-travelling uncle who worked on cruise ships, treated the whole family to a trip to Euro Disney, now called Disneyland Paris, the year that it had opened.

Her father had the camera out and nearly filmed every moment, Abi chuckled. "It was just amazing. You might not remember it [at that age] but I think having the film of it really solidified the memories."

One of her strongest memories of her visit to the park was the Main Street Electrical Parade. It's nostalgic for her and she gets a little choked up every time she sees it now. Her second visit took place about five years later when she was fortunate enough to go back with her Sunday school class. Her boyfriend at the time, who is now her husband, took her to Disneyland Paris for her 21st birthday as well.

Her uncle now resides outside of Las Vegas, Nevada which is driving distance to Disneyland. Anytime they go on a family vacation to visit him, Abi requests that they drive to Disneyland. She admits that they have visited Disneyland more than they have visited Disneyland Paris. There is one particular moment in her life that Abi remembers that impacted her joy and love of Disney.

When she was quite young, a "humungous" parcel appeared at their home, something they were not expecting. It was such a large box that Abi's mom had to stand to look inside of it. "This was especially exciting for my family because only at Christmas time and birthdays did we receive gifts, and this was out of the blue."

They soon discovered that the sender was her uncle. They opened the box to find it filled to the brim with Disney plush toys. Her uncle, who had no children of his own, collected all kinds of Disney plush toys for his niece and nephew during his travels. "My brother and I were completely over the moon. I think maybe this was one of the defining moments for us as Disney fans."

One toy in particular caught Abi's attention. It was Pongo, one of the dogs from *101 Dalmatians*. It was really supposed to go to Abi's brother Ben, but he saw that his sister had completely fallen in love with it and was kind enough to give it up for his sister to have. "He is still one of my most prized possessions in my collection because he goes way back. He's been washed so many times that I have had to use permanent marker to put his spots back on. But he is still loved nonetheless."

Her parents both own their own businesses, and her mom is in the bridal industry. She had been a dressmaker by trade, and Abi says she can appreciate the "overtly creative aspect" of that business. Being from creative parents, "we are all creative in different aspects; I think we were definitely influenced by our parents with that."

Abi collected beanie babies growing up and would take them apart, make a pattern, and create another one. Watching her mother sewing and designing and creating rubbed off on her. "It was the desire to create and make something that was truly your own," Abi shares.

Then the Disney Tsum Tsums came out. They are adorable little plush toys of popular Disney characters. The name means "stack stack" in Japanese because, well, you can actually stack them up. They are great for a collection for Abi because they don't take up as much room as the regular plush toys, and they remind her of the beanie babies she collected in her childhood.

With her desire to create and her love for certain Disney characters that were unavailable in the Disney Tsum Tsum line, "it dawned on me – why don't I make my own?" So she took one apart to make a pattern and re-stitched it up again. The first ones she made were mermaids because she loves the mythology aspect of them. Ariel was her first creation, followed by Ariel's sisters. Ariel has six sisters: Aquata, Andrina, Arista, Attina, Adella, and Alana. "I thought I would make them just for myself as part of the collection."

In 2016, her creations made their debut on Facebook, and everyone went crazy over them. She wasn't expecting the response that she received. "I kept getting messages from people asking me – would you make more?" She was reluctant at first, because she didn't have a lot of experience with them and thought they might not like them. After the mermaids she created, Abi just decided to make her favourite characters. They were received just as positively, she said.

Abi was eventually convinced to start selling her creations and now has a backlog of orders. "It's been good fun and quite fulfilling because you see how excited people are to get them." It reminds her of how excited she was to create a character that she loved that couldn't be found in the stores or at the parks.

Abi had posted on the Disney Dorks Facebook page that it had been a bumpy year for them in 2016. She and her husband Allan, had gotten married in November 2015, after being together for twelve years. They went to Walt Disney World for their honeymoon and were planning another trip in 2016 that they had to cancel when her husband became quite ill. He was unable to work for several weeks. To pass the time while taking care of her new husband, Abi turned to her Tsum Tsum creations. It also helped her cope with her husband's illness while they were homebound.

After a long road to recovery, they were finally able to take their Disney vacation, which included Mickey's Not So Scary Halloween Party. They had to take it easy and make frequent stops because Allan was still recovering, but they absolutely loved all of it. "That's one thing I like about all the parks; they all have their own flavour – there are things that are slightly different in each park and I love experiencing that and noticing it as well."

Before Abi and Allan went on their vacation, Abi decided that she wanted to give some of her Tsum Tsum plush toys away while they were visiting the park. She thought it would be fun to give some of her creations away and have people find her in the park. And it would be nice to meet some fellow fans as well. It was like a fun version of "Where's Waldo?" Someone had told her. However, finding Waldo or in this case Abi and the Tsum Tsums, proved to be more difficult than she expected.

On the last day of their vacation, a couple finally spotted Abi and she made her first Tsum Tsum giveaway. The two people that they met were from Scotland, and they lived only a couple of hours away from them. Out of the thousands and thousands of people visiting the parks that day, what are the odds of meeting two that are from your own country and live near you? Those are pretty amazing odds.

From a surprise box of Disney plush toys to her collection of Tsum Tsums, Abi's love of Disney and a desire to create something that was her own was fashioned. You can see this in her creations, which are done with a kind and generous heart. And anyone who is fortunate enough to be on the receiving end of one of these creations, is lucky indeed.

TONI'S TIME

*"It's a comfortable place. It's a happy place. Everybody
from all walks of life are there so you don't have
to feel separate. Everybody's welcome here."*

— *TONI CAMPITIELLO SMITH*

WHEN TONI SMITH WAS GROWING up, her parents would save up
for the whole year to be able to go to Florida. They would
drive down to spend *one* day at Walt Disney World while they
were in Florida. And Toni looked forward the whole year to
that single day they got to be at the park. She was fortunate
enough to visit the park five or six times before she became
an adult. Anybody who is a "Disneyphile" would have to ad-
mit that their first time was magical, Toni said. When she
talks about walking through those gates, she still gets goose
bumps. "I just always wanted to go."

After marrying her husband, who is "kind of a Disney nerd," they went to where else for the first time together? Walt Disney World, of course, for their honeymoon. It was the first time that she had stayed on the property. They stayed at the Fort Wilderness Lodge and got spoiled. "It was the best experience ever." They got the bride and groom hats, and photos with all of the characters. They returned to Walt Disney World again for their 5th anniversary, this time staying in a different hotel.

They had planned on going for their 10th anniversary as well, but their newborn and third child, Adam, had other plans for them.

Toni's children are 9, 7, and 6 years old now. Her 6-year-old son, Adam is autistic and mostly non-verbal. When he needs them, it is for a basic need of food or snuggles that he will ask for. To simply sit and have a conversation with Adam is not possible. This has been particularly hard on Toni because she loves to talk. "It's part of my personality." To have a child who doesn't talk a lot has been both frustrating and sad for her. But when he does speak, it is a pleasure to hear whatever he says. "We take every little bit that he gives us verbally."

The first time Toni went to Walt Disney World with her husband and children, Adam was 3 years old. They were a little afraid that Adam would be frightened and turn away from everything. "When you spend that much money on a vacation, you hope that it's going to be a good one."

When they arrived, Adam was a little apprehensive at first, but he didn't have a meltdown. As they went through the week, it became easier for him.

When they got on the ride It's A Small World in Magic Kingdom, they couldn't believe what they were hearing. Adam started singing the song!

After the ride, he would sing the song and inject one of his favourite words "pizza" in it. They would sing "It's a world of laughter, a world of pizza" and have a real belly chuckle over it.

The music was drawing Adam in. And it didn't stop there. At home, Adam would hum or sing the tunes of not only the attractions, but the various Disney shows too. It has become a big part of him now. "The music of Disney has stuck with him and made an impression on him." He will use it for enjoyment or as a coping mechanism to calm himself down to sort out all the sensory input coming at him.

And Toni loves to sing the songs too. When she is at her favourite attractions, the Carousel of Progress or the Tiki Room, she sings. "I don't care. I sing it every time and it's a magical experience."

So the conversation between mother and son becomes a song that is shared. It's Toni's time to connect with Adam. "He can understand it on his level and I can understand it on my level. We can come together for it, which is great."

Toni notices a positive change in Adam when they are at Walt Disney World. He is more engaging when he is there. He'll recognize the characters and he will want to go see them. While the family is waiting in line, he will engage with his family as well. Disney opens him up more and he is comfortable enough to open up. "I think that's the beauty of

Disney. It's so simple. It can be on the level of a child but it can also be on the level of an adult. It appeals to everybody of every age."

They also have everything Disney at home because it's something that Adam understands and he likes to have around him.

One day, Toni brought the Cinderella Castle home with her. She doesn't usually buy something like that because it's too expensive for her but when she is on Disney property, there is no monetary limit she adds. "If I want it, I'm going to buy it. I don't care how much it costs."

The castle caught her attention though, especially the little plaque attached to it with Walt Disney's welcome on it. She brought it home and put it up, and immediately Adam recognized it. "It was something that meant something to him. He is just drawn to things Disney."

Toni feels lucky that they can introduce their children to the same things that she and her husband had experienced as children. It's worth the cost, even if it takes a few years to save to be able to go. "We really, really like Disney," Toni says about her and her husband. They will quote things to each other and make a lot of Disney references during their conversations.

And from the sounds of things, their children are becoming huge fans themselves.

Adam is a rollercoaster kid, Toni told me. On a trip in 2016, Toni's parents joined them. Toni, her nearly 70-year-old mother and the kids went on the Mine Train ride for the first time ever. They hadn't realized that it would go so fast. The photo of them taken on the ride said it all. There was Adam with his mouth open and a huge smile on his face. He was so happy, while Toni and her mother were hanging on for dear life. "My mother looked like she was having a stroke, but Adam looked like this was fine – this was *fabulous!*" Toni laughs.

Toni's family has the opportunity to do whatever they would like to for a vacation. She feels fortunate that they can plan Disney vacations every couple of years, that they are able to afford that. "I don't think that I would want to go anywhere else. Everything is at Disney that I want."

And whether they are at home, or visiting Walt Disney World, Disney time is Toni's time to connect with her son, singing their favourite Disney songs.

DORA'S DREAM

"Honestly, I feel Disney is my favourite."

— *Dora Speck*

Dora Speck is a sweet young woman who shares positivity through her posts on various Disney Facebook pages. Born weighing only 1 lb 6 oz., she was a miracle baby and was lovingly adopted by her parents Charlotte and Willy. She was a pretty special baby – a survivor against many odds.

Despite being blind since birth, she grew up dreaming about Disney. The Canadian National Institute for the Blind (CNIB) is a volunteer agency that is dedicated to assisting Canadians suffering or living with vision loss. It was the CNIB that introduced a young Dora to the world of Disney by sending her descriptive videos of Disney movies. "They started my Disney infatuation," she says. The first movies that she was introduced to were *Cinderella* and *Dumbo*.

The music, the stories, and the descriptions in the movies had a young Dora's imagination under its spell. She's been "watching" them ever since and dreaming about a time that she could go to Disney and feel the magic that she had been told about through her movies.

After waiting nearly fifteen years, Dora's dream was about to come true.

Dora spent a year at college on Vancouver Island in British Columbia, Canada. She stayed with a family that were her "home share providers" that took care of all of Dora's needs while she was studying away from home. The family consisted of Carlien, the mother, Peter the father, and Jeremy, their 19-year-old son. They were planning a family vacation to Palm Springs in California and invited Dora to go along with them. Knowing how much she loved Disney, the family broke some exciting news to her a week before they left. They were going to take her to Disneyland for a day while they were in California on vacation!

Dora remembers that day well and quickly told me that it was Sunday May 22, 2016 when she went into the Disneyland park. They had to get up early to drive the nearly two-hour trip from Palm Springs to the park. When they arrived, the family wanted to grab a bite to eat first. But not Dora. She was too excited to eat. "So I waited ever so patiently."

When they finally arrived at the gates, it was decided that Peter and Jeremy would go to Disney's California Adventure, while Carlien and Dora would head off to Disneyland.

When Dora first walked in, she heard all the people and the music of Disney. She bought a hairband with a Minnie bow to wear because she felt that she needed something to be a part of it all. She wanted to show everyone "I'm here – this is me!" and feel like she was a part of this magical place too.

Dora picked up a handheld audio description device from Guest Relations when she got into the park. It describes actions, settings, and scene changes to help the visually impaired "see" approximately nineteen different attractions.

Unfortunately, Dora's malfunctioned. In her excitement, she forgot to test the device out beforehand. She did not go back to exchange it. It was not only time-consuming to do so, but very difficult to navigate through a large crowd at Disney, even with assistance.

Dora is not one to dwell on the negative and happily went on with her day. She managed to get on four different attractions that day: It's A Small World twice, Finding Nemo, Winnie the Pooh, and the Carousel (to get off her feet for a bit).

Although spending the day was not enough time, she was grateful that she got to go at all. Dora looks forward to the Haunted Mansion ride (she loves the sound track) and the Tea Cups (she loves spinning rides) when she goes back someday.

The characters were the best part of it all for Dora. She met Mickey and Minnie and especially had fun with Donald Duck. Dora loves the princesses as well and managed to meet up with Arial, Snow White, and Cinderella. She got to feel the fabric of their garments and it was beautiful to touch. "They all seemed unique in their own special way." She especially liked the kindness shown by Cinderella. She has been to other character experiences before, but not Disney ones. "They were very accommodating by letting me touch their faces and clothes." They wanted Dora to "see" and experience what others see and experience in the best way that they could.

Dora had a lot of pictures taken that day even though she knew that she would never be able to see them. She had an idea though. Returning home from her trip, she had a little photo album made up for her home stay family as a memento of Disney and to thank them for taking her along with them. "It's about time spent with each other and the memories. No other theme park is like it." Dora has been to other local amusement parks that can never compare. Although Disney is big, the people are not judging you Dora says. "Honestly, I feel Disney is my favourite."

Dora could feel Walt's quote that extends a welcome to all that enter through the park gates, in her heart. "I would like to go back for a week or so. My dream is to stay at a Disneyland hotel on the property." Dora's other dream is to spend her birthday (whichever that one might be) at Disney as well.

"You are never too old to set another
goal or to dream a new dream."

– C. S. LEWIS

WALKING WARRIOR

"I figured I would make my first year the
most memorable. After this, I'm going to
have to be a serious adult again."

—MARISSA PARKS

PEOPLE TELL ME TIME AND again that they feel honoured to be a part of my book series; but I assure you, it is *me* who is honoured and blessed to write the stories that they have shared with me. I have been filled with joy, sorrow and grace, while listening to such depths of these lives that I am truly privileged to write about.

Sometimes I cried over the enormity of the situation while listening to them sharing with me; I most certainly did while writing them. The following story fits all those parameters. Perhaps it is because this young lady is only a few years older than my own daughter, or perhaps it's because she is one of the bravest and most courageous persons I have ever met.

Her story covers the whole spectrum beginning with a fun-loving and relatively healthy life enjoying Disney despite her disease to staring death in its face with an eloquent grace and coming out through it all to a new lease on life that is full of hope and possibilities. Her humility and stubborn determination have served this young woman well and continue to do so. I hope I am able to capture this epic life story of Marissa Parks, who was 24 years old at the time that we spoke.

Marissa was diagnosed with cystic fibrosis when she was only 6 months old. She continued to lead a normal life as she never really felt that anything in her life was different from anybody else's, she said.

At the age of 8, she was put on the transplant list for the first time. However, it was determined that she was too healthy for a lung transplant. At that time, one had to be on the list and wait to reach the top in order to receive a new set of lungs. That wait could take years.

Despite this, she still managed to live a pretty healthy life. "I did not think that anything I did was special." Marissa even started driving a junior dragster when she was about 10 years old and retired from racing when she turned 18.

Marissa's interest in Disney started with the movies. She watched *The Lion King* every day for two years straight. She just loves the movies and didn't know what Disney really was all about at that time. It wasn't until she saw a commercial about a boy and his dad who were too excited to sleep because they were going to Disney, that she realized that it was actually a place you could visit.

Marissa's first trip to Walt Disney World didn't turn out quite as the family had expected. "I'm an expert [trip planner] now but we weren't back than."

When she was 8 years old, she was nominated for Make-A-Wish. It took a couple of years to fulfill her wish as for some reason, she had first asked for her own farm with cows and chickens, Marissa laughs. Marissa had been told that they couldn't do that, so she said, "I guess I'll go on a Disney cruise instead."

She was 10 years old when she was finally able to take her cruise. "And that's when I really fell in love with the company." It was the most incredible and magical thing that she had ever done at the time. Her favourite part was going for tea with Wendy from *Peter Pan.* It was originally supposed to be Alice from *Alice in Wonderland,* but she wasn't available at the time.

That was quite all right with Marissa; she really, really loved Peter Pan and still does today. There were other children there too, including other Wish kids. After visiting for a moment with the other children, Wendy invited several to her table. And Marissa was one of them. "It was so incredible. It was the coolest thing. I don't like tea, but I drank a lot of tea that day."

On their second trip to Walt Disney World, she happened to be in the right place at just the right time. The park was hosting the now defunct Disney channel games where celebrities would participate in teams while representing charities. Marissa begged her dad to take her to see them. While they were in Epcot that trip, her dad stayed with her while her mom and sisters went back to their hotel. They just happened upon the red carpet event for the Disney channel celebrities that was unfolding before them.

Their three hour wait was worth it. She got to meet stars like the Jonas brothers, Demi Lovato, and the Cheetah girls, whom she watched regularly on the Disney channel. "It was awesome. It was pure luck."

In 2010, Marissa and her family went on another Disney cruise. She talked with a lot of the cast members and they told her about the college program, encouraging her to try it out. *Wow, that would be perfect!* Marissa thought. And so, she did.

Marissa started the college program in August 2013. She worked as a custodial cast member working on the beach and pools at the Polynesian resort. It was her first time at a Disney resort, and it became one of her favourite places on property. On her first day of on-the-job training, her supervisor found out that Marissa had never seen the Wishes fireworks show at the Magic Kingdom. She told Marissa that the best time to clean was at 9 p.m. while the guests were on the beach watching the fireworks. Ten minutes before the show started, she told Marissa exactly where to stand to watch. She insisted that Marissa see it that evening. "It was the most incredible experience getting to watch Wishes for the first time on my very first day of work." (Coincidentally, during my final read of this story, the final Wishes show will be this evening).

Marissa never had a bad day during her college program. "You are no happier than when you are making other people happy." She fell in love with the people who work there. "It's such a unique collection of people working there to solely make people happy."

While working at Walt Disney World, Marissa found out about the Tower of Terror 10-mile run they were offering at the time. Some of her friends were going to do it and Marissa thought it would be fun do it too. It is her favourite ride and she loved the "creepiness of it." The Twilight Zone is one of her favourite shows. She hadn't trained for the run though and found that she couldn't complete it. Soon after the run in November, she got really sick. She was 3½ months into her college program and couldn't finish it, either. "It was the worst thing to happen in my life, to leave Disney." The cystic fibrosis was to blame for this downturn in her health.

While Marissa was in the hospital, she continued to train for her runs, "which sounds absurd" she quipped. She managed to walk up to seven miles a day up and down the corridors, determined to get better and determined to succeed with her running the next time!

When she is in her usual training and race mode outdoors, Marissa does a combination of a 15-second run with a two-minute walk. Most of the time though, it is a really fast walking pace. If she sees the pace setters, she will just walk faster. It is more effective for her to walk faster than to run, as it takes her too long to recover from short intervals of running.

In 2014, Marissa trained for the Tower of Terror 10-mile run, walking up to eight miles a day. She returned in 2014 to do the run and finished. "It was a really good training experience for the half-marathon."

Marissa completed both the Avengers 5K and half-marathon that year. She was not going to let cystic fibrosis hold her back. I asked her how she managed such a feat. Marissa explained that for the first couple of miles, you feel pretty good. By mile 6, you think that you are almost there, and then you realize that you are not almost there. You are not even *half-way* there yet. Then you get to mile 10 and you say to yourself, "Okay, I've got a 5-kilometer run left – only 5k more. I have done that before. You can make it. Then 30 minutes later, before you get to mile 11, you're thinking *Oh my God, mile 10 was years ago*. It's a lot harder on your mind than it is on your body," she shares.

In 2015, she set her sights on the Expedition Everest event, which involved two 5K's back to back at night, with one being a scavenger hunt in Animal Kingdom. Marissa had just gotten out of the hospital the day before she was leaving for Walt Disney World, and she felt pretty good. She completed both of those as well, but she was exhausted.

A week later, she was signed up to do the Tinkerbell race at Disneyland. It did not go as planned. It had started raining during the 5K and she had not been prepared for that. Marissa would have stopped but she couldn't find shelter from the rain. She would have had to wait until the race was over for assistance to leave the race, so she just finished it instead. She was mad at herself for assuming that it had stopped raining for the day when she awoke that morning, and thus didn't dressed properly for the weather.

Marissa ended up getting really, really sick, but attempted the 10k anyhow. Although she tried to finish it despite feeling so poorly, she just couldn't. She had to stop at mile 3. She was running a fever and was very unwell. "I should not have bothered trying that morning."

Undeterred, Marissa recovered and was back to run again the following year. In 2016, she completed the 5k Star Wars Dark Side run but unfortunately was unable to quite finish the Star Wars Dark Side 10k and half-marathon that followed the 5K.

In May of 2016, Marissa started getting sick from her cystic fibrosis and had to be put on oxygen for the first time in her life. Although she had had times when she needed oxygen to help her, she could not get her lungs' function to where they needed to be. Her oxygen levels were okay, but she was feeling poorly. Her doctor told her the numbers don't matter as much as how she was feeling.

In August things took a turn for the worse. Marissa had woken up at 3 a.m. unable to breathe properly. Even her oxygen wasn't helping. She thought she was having a panic attack with her rapid heartbeat. She had been fine the day before and had enjoyed lunch and some shopping with her mom. She couldn't figure out what was going on.

At 6 a.m. she woke her mom and told her she needed to go to the hospital. For two days, they tried to figure out what the issue was, as her oxygen levels were reading okay. The doctor assured her that they would get to the bottom of things and she probably wouldn't need a lung transplant for another year or two. She wasn't on the list for a transplant at that time. She was told not to worry, but she was going to be in the hospital indefinitely until things could be figured out and addressed.

One morning, Marissa was woken up at 4 a.m. They had finally discovered what the problem was: her carbon dioxide levels were reading at 94%! She was being poisoned. "It was incredibly bad." What made it worse was the horrific treatment from the nurse on duty. She told Marissa and her mom that there were three options. The first option was to be put on a transplant list but she said that Marissa probably wasn't a good candidate and she would have to be put on a ventilator. Option two was to just put Marissa on a ventilator to see if she would recover and to put her in a coma to take some of the stress off her body. The nurse, however, told them that she didn't think Marissa would wake up from it! The final option was to just make Marissa comfortable. "It was a horrible thing to say to us."

To top all of this off, the inconsiderate nurse wanted an answer, and she wanted it NOW.

Marissa and her mom were beside themselves. The nurse told them that Marissa had two hours or two weeks to live!

They called her dad. This needed to be a family discussion and a family decision. Her dad came immediately. They talked and basically planned the rest of her apparently shortened life. Marissa started contacting a few friends. A friend from college was in town to visit family and had planned to stop by and visit Marissa in the hospital at some point. "I didn't know how to tell my friend that I might not be there in the next few days for her to come see me."

It was 10 a.m. when Marissa's doctor came in laughing and smiling. The family couldn't believe his behaviour while they were preparing for Marissa's imminent passing. "My mom and dad were just appalled at how happy he could be, because we were in this devastation mode."

The doctor asked cheerfully, "Have you thought about anything?" They all responded "No!" and were quite taken aback. But then the doctor started to explain their choices, the *real* choices. He told them that he thought she would be a GREAT candidate for a transplant. "I didn't believe a word he had to say," Marissa said.

He wanted her to get on the transplant list right away. They were bewildered by the absolute opposite to what the night nurse had told them. The morning nurse came in and Marissa asked her what she knew about the doctor that had just spoken with them. She told the family that he was always the one to give the bad news. "I don't know if I can believe you, but I like what I'm hearing," Marissa replied.

Marissa was in pretty rough shape. They had to put her on a life support machine and had to connect it to an artery in her leg. This was very frustrating for her, because she wasn't allowed to move her legs at all in case it would dislodge the machine.

Most transplant patients can be mobile, even while on a ventilator. People help move the machines so that you can get up and walk around. Unfortunately, this was not Marissa's case. She became so weak that she could only lift her arms up for seconds at a time. She remembered trying to text when she was too weak to do that even.

I cannot imagine the agony both mentally and physically of that.

Approximately two weeks later, the hospital received a call that they may have found her new lungs. When determining if they were going to be good enough for the patient, the transplant team flies out to take a look at them. If they clear them, the surgeons themselves go look at them. They were very picky about Marissa's. Her body would be unable to handle anything less than perfect because she was so sick. The first set were not viable for her. A second call yielded the same result. Marissa's potential new lungs went to someone just a few doors down from her. The person was in fairly good health yet, and so their body would be able to adjust more easily to the lungs, unlike Marissa's.

A third call came in. However, the lungs were not in the area, so the team and surgeon had to take the hospital jet to go check them out. Marissa remembers the nurse speaking to her mom and a friend who was there at the time. Although she couldn't hear the conversation too well, she had a feeling that they had found her lungs. The scariest thing with the transplant for Marissa is that her lungs must be out by the time her new lungs arrive at the hospital. There is no down time allowed. The timing is critical for success.

At 6 a.m. they came to get Marissa prepped. They were 99% sure it would be a go. She was scrubbed down, given a sterile gown and cap, and transferred to the operating room where the prepping process was repeated. She had said goodbye to her mom and dad and her grandfathers, who were there also. "You don't know whether you are saying bye or *goodbye*," Marissa shared.

She was in the room with about 30 other people waiting for the okay to begin the surgery of removing her lungs. "At this point it's the most terrifying. It is more relieving to hear that ones aren't going to work out. It's great, but it's also completely terrifying."

While she was lying there, she heard the phone ring on a couple of different occasions. On the third ring, she heard someone answer and say, "Okay. It's a go."

Marissa panicked slightly again and thought *Oh my God.* The anesthesiologist sat beside her the whole time and told her if she was scared, she could hold his hand. And she held it the whole time as far as she knew. They started the transplant on September 2, 2016 and finished it at 1a.m. the next morning, one month from the day that she had been first admitted.

At around 7 a.m., Marissa popped right up, wide awake and ready to move. She had felt like nothing had ever happened. She was still on the ventilator as are all transplant patients when they first wake up, but she managed to convince them to remove it. It was really weird to be able to breathe,

Marissa said. The transplant had been a success! She had to remain in the hospital for rehabilitation for awhile, but Marissa wanted to be out for Halloween and worked hard to do so. She was released from the hospital just under two months from her transplant.

In the meantime, Marissa has continued with her pulmonary and physical therapy to strengthen her lungs and to help her get strong again. She had to get strong enough to be able to stand again, let alone be able to take steps due to her immobility while on life support. She has nerve damage in both her legs especially in the one that had her connected to life support. She cannot feel some parts of her feet, which is uncomfortable. She has pain at the bottom of her feet as well, which is one of the hardest parts to deal with.

The discomfort of not feeling her feet is not a big deal, she said. And she is not letting this hold her back. The day before I interviewed Marissa in early April 2017, she had walked 1.34 miles at a speed of 2.7 miles an hour!

She was back.

And there is no stopping this walking warrior who has a new lease on life and new goals to keep. She has a trip to Walt Disney World, a trip to Disneyland, and a Disney cruise booked for the upcoming year. Her goal is to complete the aptly named Super Hero half-marathon at Disneyland in November. "I figured I would make my first year the most memorable. After this, I'm going to have to be a serious adult again," Marissa laughs.

LIVING THE DREAM

"I want everyone – kids, families, anybody who loves the parks – to have a positive experience in it. That is part of why I do, what I do. That's part of what drives me."

— RIDE SOFTWARE ENGINEER, ROBERTO ROMERO

LIKE MOST OF US, ROBERTO'S first introduction to Disney was through his exposure to the Disney movies. *The Fox and The Hound* was the "baseline" for his love for Disney. He didn't grow up in the parks as a kid. As a matter of fact, his first experience visiting a Disney park mirrored my own when he visited Disneyland at the age of 12, too. The second time he went to Disneyland coincidentally mirrored mine again when he visited at the age of 19. It wasn't until he met his wife and I met my husband that we started visiting the parks regularly: he at Disneyland, and I at Walt Disney World.

During college, some of his friends really loved Disney so they would go a couple of times a year. His love for Disney continued to evolve. Roberto soon discovered that being a Disney fan was going to move to a whole new level.

Roberto met his girlfriend and was introduced to her family of hardcore Disney fans. His future mother-in-law had been going to Disneyland since its opening, and his future brother-in-law could recite all the lines from the sound track on every single attraction. They introduced Roberto to the smells of the Pirates of the Caribbean, which he said had surprised him initially. He never realized at the time that there even *were* distinct smells for the attractions and he was trying to understand this. "I'm thinking that I'm a Disney fan but then I come into this situation when the person I'm dating at the time has blown me away with that world [of Disney]."

Roberto graduated from college and had his eyes on a job in the aerospace industry. His wife had her eyes on her dream of working at Disneyland. "It wasn't that tangible (for him) to work at Disney at the time. It was more like "I need to get a job, I need to make her wishes come true." And that's what he did. He got a job with an aerospace company in California and his wife got a job at Disneyland. Often, they would meet after work to have dinner and a little fun in the park. And Roberto's love for Disney continued to grow.

Friends and family would come to see them, which led to frequent visits to the park. Roberto built up his knowledge about not only the Disney company but what the parks do as well.

In 2006, Roberto and his wife took a trip to Walt Disney World in Florida, where the update for the Haunted Mansion had just been completed. The Haunted Mansion just happens to be Roberto's favourite attraction and not surprisingly, Halloween is his favourite holiday. He attributes this to weekly library visits during his childhood when he discovered a book about the old Hollywood monster movies, detailing characters like Dracula, the Mummy, the Hunchback of Notre Dame, etc. He got right into this genre at a very young age, and this transferred over into his love for the Haunted Mansion and *The Nightmare before Christmas.*

They were with a tour guide in the Haunted Mansion that day and were told to hang back in the stretch room while everyone else went on towards the ride. It was then that they realized why they were asked to stay back. They could hear the spooky, spectral voices of the ghosts, and because of the surround sound, they were able to hear the ghosts whipping around them. It was at that moment that a "light bulb" went on. "I'm hooked. *This* is what I want to do with my life. I want to get out of aerospace and I want to go work for Disney," Roberto said that day. "I want to do these kinds of things for the public and for kids and everybody to experience and provide that kind of visceral interaction."

In 2014, Roberto would make this a reality, but it would be a long 8-year journey to get there. He applied for a couple of positions and got a call back for the second one that was identical to what he was doing for work at the time. However, the job description had literally changed overnight much to his dismay. The job number was the same, but it now required something different from what Roberto had submitted the previous day.

After being contacted by the recruiter to discuss the new requirements, Roberto had a clearer understanding about what they were now looking for. He knew what he had to do to fulfill the requirements and get the job. And he would do everything he could to prepare for it and ensure that he would get the job next time. His degree in software engineering wasn't quite enough. He also needed to obtain a certificate in industrial controls, similar to factory automation controls, which was something they didn't have in the aerospace world.

Not allowing this to deter him from his dream, Roberto sought out an Industrial Controls certificate program and enrolled at Cal State Fullerton. It was a program that would take 1 ½ years to complete.

Upon completion, however, there were no job postings listed at the time, and it would be another 18 months before Roberto would see another job opening that matched what he was seeking.

The day finally arrived when another posting appeared, and Roberto applied. He went through the interview process and got hired. He was on his way! Roberto got to work on a variety of attractions at Disneyland such as Indiana Jones, Tower of Terror, Splash Mountain, Radiator Springs Racers, and his all-time favourite: The Haunted Mansion.

Things had really come full circle for him. "I tell people if you left me in the Haunted Mansion for the rest of my career, I'm a happy man," Roberto laughed.

But Disney had other plans for him, bigger and greater plans than Roberto could ever have imagined. They saw something in him and in his work that they liked and they wanted. And Roberto was about to start living an additional dream. After just a few short years, he was invited to join the Imagineering team on the new Star Wars Land in Disneyland! "I was in utter shock."

"It was an honour to be chosen as there were a lot of people that would have loved to be a part of this. These jobs are probably *the most coveted* jobs you could ask for."

The offer was ever the sweeter because Roberto had never imagined that he would be included in a project of this magnitude. He was still relatively new and low in the hierarchy so it wasn't on his "radar," he says.

In talking to me, Roberto reflected upon where he had come from, as a Disney fan, to where he was now, as a *die-hard* Disney fan. Where at one time he couldn't fathom what smells his wife's family were referring to in the attractions, "now you could blindfold me and not tell me where you were taking me and I would instantaneously know where I was when you took me there."

When asked for advice to pass along to others who wish to pursue *their* dream to work for the Disney company, Roberto had this to say. Disney likes to hire from within. They are like any normal company requiring people with a variety of skill sets at any point in time. Of course they still pursue people from the outside, but Disney does hire a lot internally.

With this being said, he tells young people whether they are in high school or college to try to get an internship in "some way, shape or form." This should be the number one priority he states.

Secondly, like any company, he says to know their technology that they are using. Find out because the information is out there. Do what you can to understand that technology whether its through schooling or tinkering with things yourself he shares.

An unconventional yet effective interview was conducted with a gentleman Roberto had met whose hobby was building mini rollercoasters. "That's something that he brought with him to the interview [the roller coaster he built]. They were able to see what he could do and what he had a thirst for knowledge for."

Roberto's desire to create experiences that have a positive impact on guests was first sparked from his own experience in the stretch room at the Haunted Mansion. For him, it was the experience of the ghosts and spectres whereas for someone else, it could be their experience interacting with the characters or riding the attractions that have an affect on them.

He was recently on a trip to the park with friends and their 6-year-old daughter. They were on It's a Small World when he saw the little girl's reaction and how her face just lit up. He says that he wanted *everyone* to have that kind of experience; kids, families, anybody who loves the parks to have a positive experience in it. "That is part of why I do what I do; that's part of what drives me."

To be able to be a part of the creative process – to see the whole process and the final product and its impact on people is truly a privilege and a dream come true. "It's definitely not lost on me what it means, and the experience I will have in the development of this new attraction in Star Wars Land and what not. It's something you can't fathom."

Roberto was able to attain his dream through his determination and his hard work. He is now *living* that dream because of one magic moment he experienced in the stretch room, in the Haunted Mansion, in Magic Kingdom on a visit to Walt Disney World.

SOMETHING DISNEY

"It has to be something Disney."

— JONATHAN, 11

"I worry every single day – I can tell you, when I was in Walt Disney World, I didn't think about it one time, because I saw how happy my son was."

— YESENIA MCCOY

MORE OFTEN THAN NOT, I am humbled when I receive a story because there is always more to it than I first expect.

Being a mother of three, it was difficult for me at times to write this story and a few of the others I have written. As parents, we empathize with those parents that are going through extraordinarily trying times. And like most parents, we just do what has to be done to make sure our children will be okay.

I am truly grateful that Yesenia, the mother of Jonathan, was willing to share the journey that led them to their Make-A-Wish trip to Walt Disney World in 2016. But I am especially happy to know that her son beat his cancer.

Yesenia says that her children's love for Disney comes from her. She has always loved Disney and since the kids were little, "it's been Disney, Disney, Disney." In fact, she laughed, "I'm remodelling a bathroom and just ordered everything to create a Disney bathroom."

Yesenia and her family live about four hours from Disneyland and have annual passes that enable them to visit the park every other month; which they did until Jonathan received his cancer diagnosis that fateful day in September. "It was a really big change for us to not be able to go to Disneyland."

But those were the least of her thoughts at the time. As soon as they found out, she called up Disney to cancel their passes. She was concerned because she knew that Disney doesn't usually cancel annual passes. But the cast member reassured Yesenia that it was no problem at all; they were cancelled before she even hung up the phone with them. "I was really shocked at how fast and understanding they were. They were really amazing."

Their journey began in September 2015 when Yesenia noticed Jonathan was having eye trouble. She took Jonathan straight to the eye doctor. Yesenia thought that perhaps he just needed glasses, but something more sinister was at play.

After examining Jonathan, the doctor handed her a referral to Kaiser Medical Center with the words URGENT in all capital letters. The words "possible edema" were also written down. Knowing that she shouldn't really be googling anything, Yesenia went home and did anyway. She knew what it was right away – cranial pressure. Her uncle had just passed away a week earlier from brain cancer.

The next day at the hospital, they did another eye exam and CT scan. Two hours later, Jonathan was admitted to the ICU with surgery scheduled the following week to remove a rapidly growing tumour. "It's like you're fine one minute and all of a sudden, you're in ICU." A week later, the brain tumour was successfully removed.

The neurosurgeon was confident that he had gotten it all, so Yesenia and Jonathan went home to rest, recover, and await test results. The news came a week later. And their journey of great fortitude began. The results showed that he had a rare form of bone cancer. The fight began. In earnest.

For the next 10 months, Jonathan and his family went through one of the most difficult paths that a family could travel: chemo, radiation, and in his case, dozens of transfusions.

Throughout this time, Yesenia stayed with her son day and night, week after week, month after month while her husband took care of the other children – including their 2-year-old daughter.

She continued working at her job from Jonathan's bedside. "It was a really tough journey for him and for us as a family.".

While Jonathan was still in treatment, a social worker came in one day and told them that they were going to have a wish granted through Make-a-Wish. Yesenia and her family got really scared at this news. They thought that Make-A-Wish was for children with terminal illnesses who weren't going to make it; kids who were *really* sick, as their last wish.

But the social worker explained that it's also for kids who have gone through a tough illness and who have dealt with a lot. She reassured Yesenia that a lot of the children go on to live very healthy lives. Jonathan's eyes lit up and his first words were "It has to be something Disney!"

Well, there is a lot of Disney to choose from. Jonathan had always wanted to do a Disney cruise so they explored that possibility and did some research on the idea. A week later, after more thought and more discerning, Jonathan decided that he wanted to go back to Disney. He wanted to go to Walt Disney World. His reasoning behind his decision was that there were no rides on the cruise like there are in the parks, and there was no castle...

"This trip was all about Jonathan this time. He picked out the rides and decided what we did." This was more like the *something Disney* he was after.

Make-A-Wish reassured them that this trip would not only be memorable, but it would be free of any worries or financial hardships. They had a lot of medical bills to cover.

True to their word, the organization covered luggage fees and even lunch at the airport for the family. A quick check with Jonathan's neurosurgeons whether he could do rollercoasters yielded permission. They were on their way!

When the wish makers met up with them for the first time, they brought Jonathan Disney balloons, a Woody doll, a Woody shirt, a Make-A-wish button, a back pack, and a shirt. They asked Jonathan to wear his Make-A-Wish shirt as much as he could on his trip. They told him that he would get a lot of special treatment in a lot of different places if he did.

Jonathan got the Woody doll and shirt because the organization learned that this was one of his favourite characters. He has watched the *Toy Story* movies about 50 times each. It was *something Disney* that helped take this little boy's mind off of his pain and suffering during his stay in the hospital. In addition to Woody, Jonathan also loves Mickey Mouse; "Mickey is everything to him," Yesenia shares.

Right from the start, the family received royal treatment from *everyone* they encountered. They had VIP check-in, so they weren't required to stand in line at the airport. After going through security, a representative from United Airlines met them and took them to their lounge. "Don't worry about anything. I will come back and get you when it's time to board," she told them. There was a buffet of snacks, games to play, and a large window to watch the aircraft taking off and land.

When they had boarded, a flight attendant told them the captain wanted to see Jonathan. He was invited to have photos taken in the cockpit with the captain. It was a great start to a great trip!

When the family arrived in Orlando, a Make-A-Wish representative was there to greet them. "We didn't have to do anything," Yesenia said. "We walked up, got our keys, and drove to the Give Kids the World Village."

Once they arrived at the village, they had an orientation and were given three-day park hopper passes for the family to Walt Disney World and a Genie pass. This Genie pass worked its magic everywhere the family went at Walt Disney World.

Their first park was Magic Kingdom. "That's our family's number one park." As soon as cast members saw that they had a wish child, the family was taken aside and given special treatment. They were moved to the fast pass line and given preferential treatment for character meets and shows. The cast members worked hard to make the trip a wonderful and memorable experience for the family.

It was well deserved.

"It was really, really, amazing," Yesenia relays.

The first thing Jonathan asked to do was ride Space Mountain. He was so excited that day. Yesenia wished that she had brought her phone to record him. "He was just google-eyed. He was throwing his hands up in the air, his feet were going in the air, and he was yelling WOOHOO! I wish I could have recorded that. That's something that will be in my head forever."

Jonathan was the happiest she had seen him in a very long time. He was celebrating – he was celebrating life with *something Disney*.

At the end of their first day, Yesenia broke down in tears, realizing that this would be their only time to go to the Magic Kingdom. They had two days left and three more parks to visit. "I didn't want to leave."

Jonathan noticed his mom's tears. He said "You know what, Mom? We'll come back tomorrow again."

"Are you sure?" Yesenia asked him. After all, this trip was for him.

Jonathan said "yeah, we'll come back tomorrow again." This little boy's thoughts were only for his mom. He was finally able to wipe the tears from his mom's eyes that night, something he had been unable to do in the previous 10 months.

After visiting Epcot and Hollywood studios, they ended up returning to the Magic Kingdom for the last two days as well. It was a reminder of all that they had had in their times at Disneyland together before Jonathan's diagnosis. And it gave the family hope for good things to come.

Although her husband tries to reassure her that Jonathan is healthy, "I worry every single day," Yesenia said. He will have to go for CT scans every three months for the next five years. "I can tell you – when I was in Walt Disney World, I didn't think about it one time because I saw how happy my son was."

It's such a source of happiness, Yesenia tells me. When she walked into the Magic Kingdom, she would just stop, look around, and take a deep breath. It was a place for her and her family to forget everything. They didn't have to think about next month's scans because Jonathan had had cancer; they didn't have to think about any of it. They were in the Magic Kingdom. It's a place where we can forget what we have gone through and be able to be free from those fears, worries, and burdens – free to live in the moment and just enjoy.

And this is the magic of *something Disney.*

JUST DANCE

"We got to experience Disneyland a different way,
because I had more energy to spend with them."

— MELL MALLIN

I CANNOT BEGIN TO DESCRIBE how inspired I was after interviewing Mell Mallin. Not only is Mell a lovely Australian, but she is truly exemplary of what it means to overcome a phenomenal physical challenge through blood, sweat, and tears – well, maybe not the blood. And you will probably be inspired too, after you read her story.

Mell's love and desire for the Disney experience runs deep. Despite the distance, cost, and time it takes to get to the parks in North America, she tries to make the trip as often as she can. "I'm a Disney freak at the very core of my body."

Her first experience at a Disney park took place at Disneyland when she was about 10 years old. The trip was a surprise for Mell and her mother, but probably more so for her mother.

When Mell's mom was 6 years old, she used to dream about going to Disney, especially while watching the *Wonderful World of Disney* on television. She told her parents that one day she was going to go there. Her father, a Polish immigrant during the war, squashed such fancies. He told her about the cost and the distance and that she was foolish for thinking that it would ever be possible to go. But "a dream is a wish your heart makes," as the song goes. Even though Mell's mother's dream had been dismissed, it was not gone from her heart.

When Mell was about the same age herself, her dad was entering the lottery regularly. He would scrape enough money together each week to enter it together with 11 of his colleagues. They did this for three years until one day their number came up. Each of the 12 won about $10,000 which was a lot of money 26 years ago.

Her parents were wise and sat on it for a while. They spent just the smallest of amounts while trying to decide what they were going to spend it on. One day while they were out for a walk in their little town, Mell's dad pulled her mom into a travel agency and told her, "I think we're going to Disneyland." This was her mom's dream come true, and the beginning of Mell's love for Disneyland.

Mell's second trip to a Disney park happened when she had just graduated from high school. The family spent two months in the United States, one of which was spent at Walt Disney World. Since Australia's summer vacation is during Christmas, it was the perfect opportunity to see the festive decorations. With that length of stay (can you imagine?!), it was cheaper for them to buy annual passes Mell said chuckling at the memory.

Mell eventually got married and had three children before she made her third visit back to the park. Eighteen months after the birth of her third child, her dad decided that he wanted to go back to Disneyland but this time with Mell's whole family.

In 2010, the seven of them set off for their wonderful vacation. At this point, Mell had steadily put on weight, tipping the scales at 130 kilograms (286 pounds). It was the heaviest she had ever been, and it was uncomfortable for her to visit Disneyland. Mell remembered standing in line to ride California Screamin' at Disney's California Adventure park worried and thinking *I'm not going to fit on that chair.* She managed to fit after all and heard the click of the seatbelt. She was relieved, but she was very uncomfortable. She was also terrified that the buckle might not hold her in during the ride.

When she arrived back home in Australia, she made up her mind to get her weight under control.

Mell began exercising with the thought that they would be going back to Disneyland. "I was going to get on that ride, I didn't care how long I was going to wait in line. I was going to fit in it and there wasn't ever going to be a problem again."

Mell started caloric-counting along with exercising on the elliptical trainer that was "hanging around" her house.

She hopped on and her weight loss journey began. She had been on it faithfully for two weeks and could feel herself gaining more strength and felt like she was beginning to slim down a little bit. And then one day, the elliptical trainer broke; completely giving way underneath her. The weight restriction on it the equipment was 110 kilograms or 242 pounds. Mell was 20 kilograms or 40 pounds heavier.

Mell cried and contemplated giving up. After collecting herself, she realized that the two weeks of calorie counting and exercising was actually working for her. She pushed on. She wasn't going to let a broken elliptical trainer stop her. *I'm going to keep trying* she said to herself.

Without the elliptical trainer, Mell decided to start walking. After about 10 minutes of walking, she stopped. "I couldn't function anymore." *This was really hard; how can this be so hard?* she asked herself. Living in a hilly area had made it particularly difficult for such a heavy woman. Mell made it back home and cried once again.

She went to a friend's house for comfort and support. Mell explained to her friend that she wanted to work off the weight in the privacy of her own home. She felt very self-conscious that people would be judging her if she was out and about exercising. Her friend suggested to her that she should try Zumba for the Nintendo Wii.

Zumba is choreographed dancing to a variety of music. It is a lot of fun and a real workout. (I can speak from experience. It's something that I tried for a bit at our local YMCA. I say *tried,* because I was the one that was always out of sync with the instructor. The women and men that were 10 to 15 years older than me put me to shame. However, Zumba for the Wii, I will have to try!)

And that's exactly what Mell did. She continued counting calories and did Zumba Wii for about an hour every night. She wasn't watching the time as much as she was making sure that she was working up a sweat and increasing her heart rate. "I felt like I was achieving something. I really, really did." Once her metabolism had started working, she found that her interest and need to exercise turned into a desire to do so. "It was something that de-stressed me."

And that exercising and calorie counting was paying off. Mell lost an amazing 20 kilograms or 44 pounds by just dancing!

One time when Mell was getting ready to do her Zumba program, she suddenly had the urge to run. She had so much energy, she had to do more. And that was the day that Mell decided to start running. That was the day that she found out that she *could* run.

When she discovered that you could run in the Disney parks, that became a goal of hers. Mell had found a link on the Diehard Disney Nuts Facebook page to the runDisney website and discovered all the wonderful events it had to offer.

So, Mell ran. And when she ran, she thought *One day, I'm going to be running in Disneyland.*

What Mell achieved was "massive." She had planned to lose her weight over a period of two years. But in 10 months, she had lost an incredible 60 kilograms or 132 pounds! And Mell kept running.

In 2016, she signed up for Disney's virtual 5k runs, which is comprised of three separate runs, each with an allotted two weeks to get the run completed. You sign up in the limited number of spaces available, pay, and complete the runs on the honour system. You don't have to log in, and you can do the run anywhere, even walk if you chose. However, Mell did log hers. "I really wanted to slam through that." Instead of running only the three 5K runs totalling 15 kilometers, she ran 60 kilometers in 6 weeks on her treadmill!

"That was a massive deal for me and it was something that I could do without having to be in the parks." She signed up for another virtual run and is training for a 5k run at Disneyland in November 2017 when we talked, giving herself a year to prepare for it. "It's really a long way for us to go, and it's a lot of money and you just pour your heart into getting there."

When Mell is in the parks, she feels that it is the way the world should be. She sees how happy and courteous and kind people are to each other. "The cast members really treat you with respect, and I think it's nice to be able to take that to the outside." She tries to behave that way in her daily life, upholding the park's philosophy that she has fallen so much in love with.

The first trip back to Disneyland after her weight loss was a particularly memorable one for Mell. It had been four years since that visit in 2010 when she weighed 282 pounds, returning with her family nearly half that size in 2013. "We got to experience Disneyland in a different way because I had more energy to spend with them." Mell had bought some nice dresses to wear in the park as well. It was wonderful for her to be able to wear them instead of squeezing into "something" that made her feel comfortable.

It was the little things that were the big emotional things that she was able to accomplish alongside her energetic children that she would *never* have been able to do at the weight she was at before. One of the most memorable experiences from that trip happened as they were leaving the park. They had caught the Soundsational Parade that year and the music from the Mary Poppins part was still playing. Mell turned to two of her children and grabbed hold of their hands. "We just danced all the way out of the park."

She had come a long way. And Mell could *be* a kid once again, dancing and running in Disneyland.

THE MINISTRY OF DISNEY

"I don't believe I would have been ready to hear the call of God for ministry, if I hadn't been given the chance to embrace the values I had been exposed to at Disney."

— ANDY ATTWOOD OTTO

I MUST SAY THAT I was quite tickled to find out that Andy's favourite character was Donald Duck, too. I was also surprised to learn that one of his favourite rides was Carousel of Progress as well although he is still waiting for them to update the final scene. Before I was able to ask Andy why he liked Donald Duck, he asked me first. I told him that I loved Donald because he can be both crabby and loveable at the same time. Things just seem to happen to him that are out of his control. Andy then shared that he liked Donald Duck because he was so human: he gets angry, he gets frustrated, he makes mistakes, and things go wrong.

He never intends to get into trouble; he is merely misunderstood. Chip and Dale are typically the instigators. Donald Duck just goes about his business and they tease him. They deliberately upset him. "I like him because I can relate to him," he shares.

Andy Otto's story is a unique one. Unbeknownst to him at the time, his experiences on his two Disney college programs started forming his affinity for ministry. "It planted the seed for my future desire for ministry."

It all started when Andy was 5 years old on his first trip to Walt Disney World with his family. He remembers telling his parents on that trip "I'm going to work here one day." It was while he was in his freshman year at college, that he noticed a poster advertising for the Walt Disney World college program where students can obtain credits while working there. "I reverted back to my 5-year-old self and thought, *Wow! – This is a dream that can come true.*" After telling the recruiter about wanting to work at Walt Disney World since he was 5, he got the job. He began working at Casey's Corner in the Magic Kingdom in 2003.

One thing Andy remembers about that time was his trainer who told Andy and the other new cast members that they would have days when the guests were not going to treat them well. And because of this, they might feel like they were losing some of the magic. He told them to just step out onto Main Street and look at the castle. He assured them that it would bring back the magic; it would remind them of what it was all about.

Andy always reminded himself of that because he *did* experience some tough times. Being a cast member wasn't always easy. "I think this was the precursor to reminding myself that there is something higher – there is something transcendent – there is a higher purpose."

He returned to school, but he knew he wanted to do another college program. By that time, Disney had changed it slightly and offered advanced internships. Andy knew that there was one for guest relations. He wanted to work for guest relations as that had been one of his next dreams. "It was kind of the thing [to do] for a lot of people to wear the plaid and wear the *D* pin."

Andy applied. Out of the 100 applicants, he was one of the 15 to get the job. He was thrilled by this, he says. "I am passionate about Disney and I really care about the guest experience. A lot of people don't realize the impact they have on these guests who have saved for years to bring their family; they have such high hopes for sharing this magical experience with their families."

Most of the Disney roles, including those at the attractions, represent a character. Andy told me that the character affiliated with guest relations was Mary Poppins. He would often think of himself in that role; "I have something here to help you to meet your needs." The ability, and the opportunity, to be with guests in their moments of joy and sorrow in what they were experiencing requires empathy and taught him to be a good listener Andy said. He had to learn to really listen to them and respect where they were at, and try to help them in whatever way that he could. He believes that it was his work at guest relations in particular that created "the little spark that blossomed into ministry."

If you had told him in 2004 that he would be going into ministry, "I would have thought that you were mad," he exclaimed. But looking back on all of it, he can see that it made perfect sense. "I can see [now] the hands of God working and instilling in me certain values and experiences that would be integral in what I've become and equip me to be a minister to people. You often see His work when you reflect back, rather than when you are in the moment."

I have to agree. We often do not realize that everything in our present moment shapes our future until we are there. And without further ado, here are the experiences and the lessons learned that led Andy to his life's work in ministry in Andy's own words.

FAMILY

My parents have always taught me the importance of caring for family, but each day at Disney, I saw hundreds of families being intentional about their togetherness. They tried to ensure they were having a good time. Couples held hands as they strolled down Main Street. Family reunion groups snapped photos with their relatives to preserve memories. The importance of family bonds was evident all around me. Walt Disney's dream was that there could be a wholesome place families could enjoy together. If I was ever having a tough day, I could look on the families and be reminded of the magic of Disney.

Disney taught me that family is priority, and that it should transcend financial hardship, disputes, and even distance.

HOSPITALITY

*Disney taught us that we should always treat each guest "as a cherished friend" and that even if the line was long, the most important person was the one in front of us; we gave them our full attention. The value of courtesy was always put above efficiency. I remember that our training taught us to be like Sneezy, one of the seven dwarfs. "Greet and welcome each and every guest. Spread the spirit of hospitality." My interaction with guests at Disney was the initial spark for my future ministry. I only realised that years later. Ministry requires your full attention to be with the person before you. I took this lesson into my work as a hospital chaplain. Sometimes my patient list was so long that if I focused solely on checking visits off the list, then I wouldn't be able to spend quality time with any of them. **Ministry requires hospitality.** Each person we encounter has dignity and worth, so we ought to receive them lovingly, making a welcoming space for them.*

*Another opportunity for ministry was volunteering for Give Kids the World, which has a resort in Orlando. The children staying there have a terminal illness, and for many of them a trip to Disney was their last wish. I volunteered some nights to hang out with the kids while their parents had a date night. It was my first experience being with children who were dying. They had such joy and innocence. **I felt within me a yearning to always love the vulnerable among us, not only a given for ministry, but a given for being a Christian.***

EMPATHY

In my second program at Disney, I worked in Guest Relations, which meant I would often have to exercise my listening skills, which was another critical ministry skill. Guests would share with me their compliments and complaints. As in ministry, my role was to share in their joys and sorrows. I'd either smile and affirm the great experience the guest was having, or I would nod and acknowledge how their experience was not so good. Families spend a great deal of time saving to make a trip to Walt Disney World so it's understandable that they might be disappointed when their expectations are not met. My primary role was not to make the experience right, but to listen empathetically. Empathy places ourselves in the shoes of the other. Empathy reminds the other that we share in their humanness. This is a skill that I have developed through the years that I apply to my ministry.

JOY

It may seem that Disney manufactures an artificial happiness – we were told to make happiness for our guests. And while that may be partly true, Disney leaves room for the other realities of life: the human struggle between good and evil, the difficulty in making good moral choices, and even the grief we deal with. Still, the human yearning for joy underpins all that Disney does, and it should also underpin ministry. As Christians, our hope is joy. We know that like a Disney story, the sorrow and suffering is only temporary. Our yearning for joy is a sign of our longing for God. The nuance in my Disney lesson though is that we mustn't always try to escape the difficulty and force joy. We must be naturally able to recognize the joy that lies beyond the fog.

DIVERSITY

*An essential element of good ministry is being a non-judgemental presence for another. We must meet each person where they are and as they are. Disney was a wonderful place to learn about the value of diversity. I had the chance to meet and work with people from many countries, with different cultures, sexual orientations, religions, and life experiences. **I could not be sheltered from the vivid diversity of the human family.** It was no longer fair for me to approach someone with my mind already made up about them. I had to literally follow Christ's command to love my neighbour, no matter who they were.*

FAITH

Disney movies have always been saturated with spiritual and moral themes. The parks too have not typically shied away from their Christian influence, thanks to Walt Disney's devout Christian background. He even had Disneyland dedicated by a reverend. Each year, Walt Disney World hosts the Night of Joy. A weekend of Christian bands playing throughout the Magic Kingdom park. The Christian influence is most apparent at Christmas time. Amid the secular Christmas songs, you'll hear traditional tunes and discover the Christmas traditions from around the world.

Each year, Epcot puts on the Candlelight Processional where a celebrity narrator re-tells the scriptural story of Christ's birth while a mass choir sings traditional Christmas songs accompanied by an orchestra. The tradition began in Disneyland in 1958 and continues today in both parks. I had the chance to sing in the cast choir for the Candlelight Processional. I'll never forget standing on the risers singing "O Holy Night," gazing at the lighted Christmas tree behind the audience, felling so blessed that I believed what I was singing about Christ. Truly he taught us to love one another. His law is love and His gospel is peace. All that existed and all the opportunities I've had, including my time at Disney, was because of this story of Divine love.

Disney became for me a sign of God, shaping me in these values that were so important to my later ministry and relationships. I don't believe I would have been ready to hear the call of God for ministry if I hadn't been given the chance to embrace the values I had been exposed to at Disney.

— Andy Attwood Otto

YOU'VE GOT A FRIEND IN ME

*"I'm so blessed. I can do what I love every day...
and have incredible experiences because of it."*

— WALT DISNEY WORLD RADIO'S LOU MONGELLO

WHEN I THINK OF LOU Mongello, the song "For He's a Jolly Good Fellow" comes to mind. He is a good "fellow" and a pretty happy one at that. What struck me after speaking with Lou was not only his friendly disposition but his indisputable work ethic. There is no doubt in my mind that this powerful combination is responsible for the life he has created for himself and his Disney family. And it all started with his love for Disney.

Lou, like so many of us, grew up watching Disney on television on Sunday nights with his parents. He was incredibly fortunate as a kid he said, because he first started visiting Walt Disney World mere weeks after it had opened in 1971. "We hopped in our 'truckster' and drove from New Jersey to

Walt Disney World." He was too young to remember that trip but he relishes the photographs taken of him and his family on Main Street USA. From then on, the family would drive down to Walt Disney World every year. Even if it wasn't their final destination, the family would always make a point to stop in for a visit. "I have incredible memories as a kid growing up at the park. I am a 7-year-old kid trapped in a 48-year-old body" he said, laughing.

And as Lou got a little older, he became fascinated with Disney. His favourite souvenirs were not the plush toys, but the books that he could read over and over, and the post cards that took him back to that magical place once again. One particular book Lou remembers fondly was a big black book from the 1970's, similar in size to the D23 book we have today. "I read that from cover to cover every day."

His fascination with Disney grew, as he grew. He started to visit the park more often, puzzling over what it was exactly that would bring people back, what this "thing" was that not only brought him back, but millions of other people back as well. His quest to find that answer is what would ultimately make him who he is today.

Lou read every Disney book that he could get his hands on. He spoke with cast members at length, even riding the monorail with the pilot until the parks closed, "probably bothering that poor cast member asking him questions." He wanted to learn *everything* that he could about Walt Disney World. He realized that *this place* was different and more special than anywhere else he had gone before.

After college, Lou went on and obtained a law degree. In addition to practicing law, he had an IT consulting company on the side. Needless to say, he didn't sleep very much. Lou's passion for all things Disney took a back seat and became his hobby. "You know, you go to school, you go to college, you go to law school and you become a lawyer. Then you do what you love on the weekends. But I learned that you don't have to live that way."

After watching too many late-night infomercials Lou chuckles, he got the idea to write a book. Being in the service business, Lou wanted to create something once and re-sell it. "I had all this…knowledge rolling around in my head… about Disney." There was no trivia book about Walt Disney World out there at that time. He also wanted to write a book that he himself would like to read. And this is what started it all – everything you see of Lou Mongello, the author, podcaster, speaker, and coach, started from a book. Little did he realize what that first book would lead to.

After completing his book, he received 47 rejection letters from publishers and one acceptance letter. "You only need one yes, and I got my yes." When the book came out in 2004, Lou had thought that "that would be it." He ended up signing a three-book deal with his publisher. And he was off.

The book was the springboard to a website, articles, and eventually podcasts, coaching, and speaking engagements. In 2005 Lou had heard about podcasting and he saw an opportunity. "The power of the spoken word was so much more powerful than I could write," he shared. And so began his podcasting.

At this point, Lou was travelling back and forth between New Jersey and Florida working hard and doing what he loved, continuing to build his brand. It was in 2007, that Lou thought *You know, I think I've got something here.* And he realized that in order to have the most accurate information for his books and podcasts to share with others, he needed to be in Florida near Walt Disney World.

With the support of his wife, Lou left his job as CTO of a medical imaging company, sold his house, packed up his Honda Odyssey, and moved to Florida into a house "sight unseen." He credits his success to his wife's faith in him and his faith in himself. "When someone says I know you married a lawyer, but I'm going to give all of this up and go write for Disney for a living, and they say 'Okay, I'm with ya,' there is not a price you can put on the importance of that support."

Many people think that Lou is lucky. "I'm not lucky – I'm fortunate," he said. "People do not see what goes on behind the scenes. They see the final product only." He works seven days a week and although, like anything, it involves sacrifice, he loves it.

I think when you find your passion and you get to do it as your career, it doesn't *feel* like work per se. "It is not easy," Lou states, "but it is a lot of fun."

"Staying hungry," determining what he will accomplish next, improving upon things and ensuring that the "ship he is steering" is taken care of, is his motivation. "You can't get complacent; good enough is *not* good enough."

Lou has a different appreciation for his life and career, which has changed significantly. He is a positive person and he leads a positive life in everything that he does, but it's the show that catapulted him into the success that he is today. "It literally changed my life, not just in terms of where I live geographically or what I do to keep mac and cheese on the table – but it changed my life in terms of my level of happiness and the ways that I approach things. It's the friendships and the relationships that I've made."

As a matter of fact, this is why he guest speaks, works with entrepreneurs, and coaches in addition to hosting his podcasts at WDWRadio.com.

Lou has gotten to experience things that he couldn't have imagined. One of these experiences includes an interview with the one and only Julie Andrews. "I lost my marbles because that's who I grew up watching with my parents. Oh, my god, Mary Poppins is at my ear," he shared with me.

He also hosts a running team that participates in the runDisney marathons. In 2007, Lou had a cohost for the show. He had been raising money to give to the Make-A-Wish Foundation of America and his cohost had laughed at the thought of Lou running in anything to help raise some of it. "I'm like, game on, brother," Lou said to him. Meeting that challenge, Lou, his wife, and a friend signed up to run their first half-marathon together. He thought it was "won and done."

However, after others got wind of it and thought if "short, skinny little Mongello can do it" (his words, not mine!) then they could do it, too. And they would be running to help support a charity as well. This was the birth of the WDW Radio Running Team. It has grown to about 700 members from all over the world, a team of people who want to run together and help support the Make-A-Wish Foundation. To date, they have helped raise more than a quarter million dollars for the charity.

As time goes on, Lou's wife has gotten more involved with what he does and more specifically on the running and charitable side of things, "which are really some of the most important parts of this whole endeavour."

Lou is the same fellow you meet in person as he is on the show. He shares quite a bit from his personal life and considers his Disney community not as fans, but as family. And listening to his program *In the Box*, he has *a lot* of extended family. "I am very transparent in *who* I am and the *life* I lead because you can't be one person on the microphone and a different one in real life. You need to be genuine. And people appreciate it more when they see that you *are* the same person. It is important to make sure that people know that you are an approachable person."

Lou conducts monthly meet ups at Walt Disney World so that he has an opportunity to meet his Disney family. He wants to be able to look them in the eye and shake their hands and give them a hug. He wants to thank them for giving him the opportunity that enables him to do what he does.

"I'm so blessed; I can do what I love every day and it doesn't feel like work and I have incredible experiences because of it." Lou has not lost the "magic" of the Disney experience, despite living in the middle of it. He doesn't go to the parks every day, but he and his family still find it exciting and fun when they do. "It's still a treat when we go."

"It's all about the food," he said, chuckling when I asked him why he returns again and again. Then he got serious. "It's really about the emotional connection that we have; you forget about everything that goes on in the real world and about everything that stresses you allowing you to be a kid again. People are different at Disney – we treat each other differently than on the regular street. I think that's why we go back; it's because of the escapism, it's the cast members – it's the expectation that's so high yet I think always exceeded."

Lou says he's a *nostalgic*. He loves the classic attractions and characters alike, so its no surprise that Peter Pan is his favourite character. What's more, he believes that Peter Pan is the best character *ever*. And the lawyer in him had this to say to back up this sentiment: "Peter Pan never has to grow up, he lives on a private island, he gets to hang out with his friends and play all day, he battles pirates and wins, he's got this little magical pixie as his sidekick, he's very, very popular with the ladies, all the mermaids love him, he's a snappy dresser, and he never has to grow up. He never, *ever*, has to grow up."

Hmmm. I don't know about you readers, but I'm beginning to see a few parallels here!

Like all of us, it is important to have friendships and relationships that have both meaning and purpose in our lives. Lou has been a pivotal and positive force in facilitating friendships from far and wide, friendships that would never have been if not for him. And anyone who has connected with him in some way, shape, or form knows that he values these relationships, these friendships he has with others. Lou, the feeling is mutual. Thank you for all that you do, sharing the magic with your Disney family.

SEEING MICKEY

"When he came to me and took me to the middle of the room, I did not know how to react. But he took my hand and when he was running my hand over his face, it made me remember my childhood."

— BASILIO SANTANA

"Everything had to be explained to him so that he could imagine what we were looking at – I had to go with him everywhere. That was incredible."

— NATALY PACIFICO WHITE

"When you get someone as unique as [Basilio], it's a pretty special thing to watch. It's really cool to know that everyone has a story and their own reasons for being there."

— TIMOTHY GILL

SOMETIMES A STORY COMES ALONG that touches people to their core, not because of the words spoken but because of the words not spoken. It was in the silence and through the actions that evoked such powerful reactions that they broke through all political, ethnic, demographic, and language barriers. How was this achieved, you might wonder? Through the undeniable universal truth of love and kindness shown to us in a young man's experience at Walt Disney World. It's the story of the power of love and kindness that transcends all languages that was shown to a young Brazilian man named Basilio Santana by Mickey Mouse himself.

I hope with all my heart that I can capture this most amazing moment in time with my words so that you can relive this exceptional moment that still pulls at my heart and the hearts of thousands of others, too.

When I first connected with Nataly Pacifico White, I discovered that she had been the tour guide for Basilio's group from Brazil. Originally from Brazil herself where she practiced veterinary medicine, Nataly now resides in Orlando with her husband and works as an independent tour guide. I was put in touch with Basilio by Nataly and despite the language difference (he speaks Portuguese and I...do not), we were able to communicate. Basilio also has a special translator that made it possible for us to email each other, and Nataly was fantastic at translating what we needed in order for the story to be told in its entirety. And for that, I am grateful to her for taking the time to do this.

When Nataly woke up that morning, she could never have imagined how special her guests that day would turn out to be. She would be responsible for one hundred people in the Magic Kingdom, and Basilio and his mother were among them. However, Basilio was not like her usual guests, for he is blind. "Everything had to be explained to him so that he could imagine what we were looking at – I had to go with him everywhere. That was incredible," Nataly shares.

Spending that much time with Basilio and his mom, Nataly learned a lot about them and she became quite taken with the story of his life. Basilio was born in Bauru, Sao Paulo State, Brazil in 1995. He was a healthy baby boy who developed into a fine young boy and enjoyed the Disney cartoons like everyone else his age. Unfortunately, in 2002, when Basilio was just 7 years old, his brother passed away. Two years later, at age 9, Basilio lost his sight literally overnight. There were many doctors consulted, medical examinations and remedies prescribed, trying to figure out what had happened and help him regain his sight, but to no avail.

In 2005, when he lost movement in his left leg, it was discovered that he had Devic's disease, a variant of multiple sclerosis. With treatment and therapy, his leg regained mobility but his sight never returned.

In 2007, Basilio sadly lost his dad to prostate cancer. Then his mom was diagnosed with Devic's disease as well. Over the next years, Basilio had additional health issues recurring from his disease. With the indomitable spirit of a fighter and survivor, Basilio did not let his illness nor his blindness keep him down, keep him from succeeding, keep him from *living* his life. He finished high school and a technical web programming course without missing any of his schooling.

To help him get through things, Basilio would tune into Radio Metropolitana FM in his city. It was there that he found the Chupim comedy show. "The radio remains my strength to go through many problems of day-to-day life," Basilio shared. In 2015, an airplane called *the Chupim* was launched that would take the members of the comedy group, the Metropolitan FM team, and guests to Orlando to visit Walt Disney World. *A chance to visit Walt Disney World?! That would be a dream*, Basilio thought.

Basilio had watched all the cartoons and movies until he had lost his sight. It was from this that his love for Disney began. Although his favourite character was Mickey Mouse, there was a lot of Donald Duck in his house too. One of his fondest Disney memories happened when he was just 5 years old. There was a special event called "In the Kitchen with Mickey and Minnie" at a nearby mall. His mom took him and he got a picture taken with Mickey and Minnie in a kitchen.

He had always known about the existence of the parks, but it was not affordable for them to go. Finally, in 2015 he and his mom went to a travel agency to check out the prices and find out what a trip to Walt Disney World would entail. But they were afraid to go alone.

So when the opportunity arose to go with a group from their own country aboard the Chupim, they were on it! Basilio signed up and bought his ticket immediately. In fact, he was the first one to do so, and his mom was the second. They had a wonderful trip.

A year later, an additional plane was launched called *the Metropolitan,* and another trip to Orlando and Walt Disney World was organized. There was a promotion for a complete trip with all expenses paid for the number one listener who had been the first to buy the previous package. He hadn't known at the time that he had been the first to purchase a ticket on the previous trip. "My mother and I were taken from Bauru to the capital by San Paolo Metropolitana FM on June 1, 2016. After arriving at the radio station, we learned that we had won the all-expenses paid trip. We were so excited. We had really wanted to go back to Walt Disney World," Basilio says.

It was at this juncture that Nataly, their tour guide, entered their lives.

They were having a wonderful time, but Nataly wanted to make it extraordinary. She wanted Basilio to meet his favourite character, Mickey Mouse; the *talking* Mickey Mouse. The only place you can find him is in the theatre on Main Street USA in the Magic Kingdom.

"When I was waiting to meet Mickey, I was pretty anxious. I wasn't too sure what was going to happen or how things might turn out," Basilio shares. He had always liked Mickey and the Mickey Mouse show that he'd watched when he was still able to see.

"When I entered the room, I was *thrilled* and very happy." And then, one of the most magical moments happened, touching the lives of all those around to witness it, and those of us from afar that saw the recording of it.

Basilio was told that Mickey was coming and suddenly, Mickey reached for Basilio's hand. He gave it an encouraging squeeze and carefully held it while leading Basilio slowly to the center of the room. Without letting go, Mickey gently clasped both of Basilio's hands and placed them on top of his head. Guiding those hands, Mickey brought them to his ears, his nose, his mouth, and then on to his hands and clothes allowing Basilio to slowly explore what Mickey Mouse "looked" like. You could have heard a pin drop. The cast members and Nataly and Basilio's mom were witnessing a beautiful connection where Basilio was able to *see* Mickey Mouse for the very first time in his life.

"I did not notice the passing time," Basilio shared. "When he came to me and took me to the middle of the room, I did not know how to react. But he took my hand and when he was running my hand over his face, it made me remember my childhood."

Basilio's mom soon joined him and Mickey. This woman who had lost so much but in that moment, had gained so much cried in Mickey's arms and said, "Thank you, I love you, thank you." And Mickey held on to her and let her cry tears of sorrow and tears of healing. "It was unforgettable for me," Basilio said.

There were no dry eyes in that room that held five cast members, a tour guide, a mom, her son, and Mickey Mouse himself. "Mickey hung on to her, and the photographer was crying and all the cast members were crying," Nataly said. She recorded the moment on her phone, and you can hear Nataly crying as well. Basilio told Nataly, "I could *feel* all of your energy – all of you in the room."

The photographer there that day was a man named Timothy Gill, who had been working for Disney for the previous three years. Along with him was his friend and fellow cast member Javier. They still talk about it and think it was pretty cool that they got to experience that together. "My favourite place is with Mickey [in the theatre] because with him, you never know who is going to walk through that door," Timothy said. "Mickey is kind of like a universal language, like Disney – like a feeling," Timothy says.

To see Basilio learn what Mickey looked like and see the connection and understanding was powerful, Timothy said. "I was crying, everyone was crying, I just kept snapping photos." He normally takes anywhere from five to ten photographs at one time, but that time he took fifty. In a day with Mickey, he takes an astounding four thousand photographs! Every day is different, there is something that happens every day Timothy says. "When you get someone as unique as [Basilio], it's a pretty special thing to watch. It's really cool to know that everyone has a story and their own reasons for being there," Timothy says.

"Basilio, he is amazing," Nataly said, "he touched a lot of people."

He has indeed.

THE REAL PRINCESS TIANA

"She still controls the kitchen. Even at
93, she is still as sharp as a tack, very
witty – fully there. She was so sweet ."

— JOE BELL

I LOVE TO LEARN ABOUT the hidden gems of the places that I travel to and particularly if they are attached to something Disney. Joe also likes to find out about things to see and do when he travels, especially if it happens to tie in with Disney as well. When he and his fiancée Rebekah, decided to visit New Orleans, a mere three-hour drive from their home, Joe started checking out what they could see and do there. You can only imagine Joe's surprise when he stumbled upon the word Disney attached to the city of New Orleans while doing his research. "It just leaped off the page when I saw it."

Joe Bell has a special place in his heart for Disney; he is a cast member at his local Disney store. He works part time there in addition to his full-time work and absolutely adores his job. I could hear his voice light up every time he shared one of his experiences while working at the Disney store. "It's all joy and love. Don't get me wrong; we're constantly moving; we're replenishing, and straightening, but what it is, is a lot of fun."

With Joe's interest piqued, he looked further into the connection between Disney and New Orleans and discovered that the inspiration behind the lovely Princess Tiana from the movie *The Princess and the Frog* was, in fact, because of a now 94-year-old lady named Leah Chase of the Dooky Chase Restaurant.

Ms. Chase and her jazz musician husband Edgar "Dooky" Chase II started working at the lottery stand owned by Dooky's parents where they also sold homemade po'boy sandwiches. Ms. Chase was no stranger to hard work having held a variety of jobs since she was very young. Through the dedication and hard work of Leah and her husband, they were able to inherit the lottery stand and eventually turned it into the sit-down restaurant that it is today. It has served celebrities and Disney executives and even boasts having served two presidents. Ms. Chase still presides over the kitchen, keeping an eye on *everything* that goes on.

The restaurant offers a buffet lunch Monday through Friday with an additional dinner served early on Friday evenings. Joe and his fiancée were amazed at the food.

"Everything tasted incredible. It was truly amazing food. Since Ms. Chase still controls the kitchen; when the fried chicken comes out, it's got to be crispy on the outside and juicy on the inside."

Ms. Chase is a huge supporter of civil rights and the arts. The restaurant's interior is covered with the artwork of local African American artists. "It's just really gorgeous inside," Joe shared. Ms. Chase is a legendary New Orleans chef, author, and television personality known as the "Queen of Creole Cuisine."

After they were seated, Joe asked the waiter if Ms. Chase happened to be there that day by chance.

Looking at Joe, he smiled and replied. "Yes sir, she's here every day."

Joe asked if it would be possible to say hello and meet her. The waiter told them it would be no problem at all. When they had finished their meal and paid up, they could let the staff know and they would be escorted back into the kitchen to meet her.

Joe could hardly wait. After their lunch, they went back to the kitchen where they spotted Ms. Chase at a little table in the center of the kitchen. She stood up to greet them.

"She was so sweet," Joe recalls.

Ms. Chase took one look at Rebekah and said, "Oh my gosh, you've got a beautiful one here!" And then she looked over at Joe and said, "You don't look so bad yourself," Joe chuckled. "She is still as sharp as a tack, very witty – fully there."

The story behind all of it goes back to when some Disney folks went to New Orleans to embrace the culture and find inspiration for a new princess for an animated film that would star an African American princess in New Orleans. They found Leah and spoke with her for hours, listening to her telling them her story. And we all know what came of those conversations...

In conjunction with the movie, Ms. Chase also contributed her Yumbo Gumbo recipe to *The Princess and the Frog: Tiana's Cookbook*, a book of recipes for kids, which I happen to own and hope to have signed when I visit the restaurant in the summer of 2017.

Joe and Rebekah stood in the kitchen speaking with Ms. Chase for about twenty memorable minutes. She signed menus for them, including one for a fellow cast member named Natasha whose favourite character is Tiana. "She was just so thrilled and happy to do it for us," Joe says.

Ms. Chase was smiling when she shared a funny story with them about a little boy who was really excited to meet Princess Tiana. When the little boy came in, Ms. Chase said he saw an old woman and stopped. Surprised, the little boy said to her with dismay, "You don't *look* like Tiana!"

It is this experience with Ms. Chase and others that has Joe fully embracing Disney. He loves visiting Walt Disney World as well and finds that as he gets older, he takes it at a different pace. He likes to slow down and really look around the park at the artistry, the artwork, and everything they put into it to make it so wonderful. He feels that there is something there that taps into that inner child that allows us to have fun. He is happy to be a part of the Disney family as a cast member, a Disney ambassador if you will, at a Disney store. "This way, I can participate in the magic and keep my [own] magic intact as well when I go to the parks."

Joe has experienced several memorable moments during his time as a cast member for Disney. But the time he got to meet Ms. Chase, aka Princess Tiana, is one that he will always remember. "It was absolutely wonderful – the whole experience, and meeting her."

I can only imagine.

After all, it is not every day that you can meet a legend *and* a princess.

DISNEY DREAMS FOR EVERYONE

*"The magical part of the whole trip had to be
the cast members; they make the magic. They
put their heart and soul into their job. That
was the magic we will never forget."*

— SARA SLADE

*"All the people looked really happy to be
there. It was just incredible to be there."*

—SOPHIE SLADE, 13

THE SLADE FAMILY HAS EXPERIENCED more than their fair share of
health crises in the last five years. Their daughter Anna was
diagnosed with diabetes at the age of 5. Daughter Sophie was
diagnosed with a connective tissue disorder requiring difficult surgeries and a heart issue. With medication however,

the future looks bright and will hopefully prevent Sophie from requiring heart surgery in the future. In addition to this Sara, the girls' mom, has a sister Ann who is a cancer survivor, and a brother-in-law Bill, who received a recent devastating diagnosis of cancer as well. "It's been a crazy couple of years," Sara said

Just after Sophie's second knee surgery, Sara decided to reach out to the Make A Wish Foundation of America without Sophie knowing. "I didn't want to get her hopes up in case it didn't work out." Sara was driving home one day when she noticed a telephone message had come in. She quickly found a place to pull over and played the message. "Everything just froze inside. I couldn't believe what I was hearing." They found out that Sophie would get her wish! Sophie, her parents, and siblings were going to Walt Disney World!

It was then that Sophie requested a modification to her wish. She knew that her Aunt Ann and Uncle Bill were having a tough year. She also knew that they had always dreamed about going to Walt Disney World. Sophie wanted her aunt and uncle to go, even though she believed by doing so that she herself "probably couldn't go" then.

Never underestimate the magic behind the Wish Makers, nor the selfless and thought-full love and wish of a child. Because dreams are for everyone, especially when they involve Disney.

"I never will forget the day that we found out that they were sending *everyone* – it was so crazy!" Sara said.

Sophie remembers that day too. They were to meet their Wish Makers, Chad and Whitney, at the Texas Roadhouse Restaurant near their home. When they walked in, there were beautiful flowers on the table. "It was very cool," Sophie said. It was then that they found out that her aunt and uncle and her whole family would be able to go. "I couldn't sleep that night – it was too incredible," Sophie shared.

"It was a very abnormal wish and I don't know how the Make-A-Wish Foundation and Disney did it," Sara said. "All *nine* of us were going to Walt Disney World." The only stipulation was that Ann and Bill had to stay at a nearby hotel while the rest of them stayed at the Give Kids the World Village. However, they could participate in any of the activities there with Sophie and her family. "It was just so incredible. It was amazing how everything just fell into place," Sara says.

So off they went: Sara and her husband Sheldon, their children Joseph, Anna, Sophie, and Myrna, and Ann and Bill on the trip of a lifetime.

They arrived April 1, 2016 (no fooling). One of the highlights of the first day they were there was meeting John Stamos, who is a frequent visitor to Give Kids the World Village. "It was so wonderful to see him," Sara said.

The first park they visited was the Magic Kingdom. "All the people there looked really happy to be there and it was just incredible to be there. We had a lot of fun walking in the parks," Sophie shared. The first stop at the park was for 8-year-old Myrna, to pick out her long-anticipated autograph book. They looked at several of them as there were many different kinds to choose from. The one that Myrna wanted was the fancy princess one but they decided on something else and "she was thrilled," Sara said. The family's adventure was about to begin, and "we had huge experiences."

The highlight of the trip happened the day that they went to Hollywood Studios to see the *Frozen* Sing-Along. Myrna was dressed up as Elsa that day. While waiting in line to be admitted to the show, the girls were especially excited. Aunt Ann in the meantime, struck up a conversation with the cast member tending to their area. She happened to mention that this was the highlight of the whole trip. The cast member had seen that the Slade family had a Wish child and asked them to wait where they were until everyone else had gone in.

Finally, the family was brought around to the front and seated. They were asked if they could wait after the show for a little bit. They said sure, of course they could! Sara teased Myrna that they were probably going to be asked to clean up after the show. "We didn't want to get her hopes up, as we weren't sure what might be in store for us," Sara shared. As Elsa and several of the cast members made their way out to the stage during the show, they would wave to the girls. "We were so surprised." When the show was over, everyone filed out except for the Slade family. About five minutes later, the stage manager came out and asked if they would like to meet the cast.

Would they!

They couldn't believe it! They met Elsa, Anna, Kristoff, and the two story tellers. They all took the time out to greet and speak with the family. "It was the coolest thing," Sara said. They even gave the girls a signed Elsa doll. "We were all in tears...we were floored that they would take the time out to do that."

There were so many experiences about that trip that the Slade family will never forget.

Halfway through the trip, Myrna had unfortunately lost her autograph book. She was devastated. They bought her a new one at a souvenir outlet nearby so that she could continue to get autographs. The depth of that loss was not lost on a little girl of 8, because on their last night at Magic Kingdom while walking through the Emporium, little Myrna had a meltdown when she realized they were not going to find her original autograph book after all. Heart- wrenching sobs could be heard by many, and to try to ease her broken heart, Sara's family tried to find something, anything that might help placate her and heal Myrna's broken heart.

One of the cast members found out what was going on and asked if they could remain where they were for a moment. Upon returning, she asked which autograph book Myrna had lost. They showed the cast member, and to their astonishment, the cast member picked out a different and more expensive book and asked Myrna what she thought about it. Myrna didn't realize the intention of the cast member at first. But when she realized that she was being *given* the book, her face went from tears to a huge, huge smile.

"My husband and I were just in tears. The manager came over and they were the first autographs Myrna wanted in her book. They were so wonderful and we all got our pictures taken with them," Sara shares.

When Sara thinks about their time at Disney, it seems surreal to her and her family. "As busy as they are and as much as people think that it's corporate, they really empower their cast members to go above and beyond." The Slade family is especially grateful to all the cast members who went out of their way to make sure that they had a great time. They were well taken care of. "The magical part of the whole trip had to be the cast members. They made the magic. They put their heart and soul into their job. That was the magic that we will never forget."

The Slade family could not believe all that had happened to make their trip be what it was. They recognized that there were a lot of hands at play to make Sophie's wish come true. "You can tell the cast members love it; they're happy and they are just some of the best people I've ever met." They could feel the spirit of everyone involved that allowed them to forget all the health issues and heartbreak that went along with those issues. They were able to focus on the present, on "we are here and life is good – it's wonderful. It was amazing – that whole trip was just amazing – just incredible."

It is through the beauty and versatility of that magic that brought not only the dreams of a girl name Sophie forth, but through her selfless love for her aunt and uncle, were able to bring forth dreams for everyone.

A HOPE AND A DREAM

*"I think she would be very proud to see
we are a part of that magic."*

— MIKE FLYNN

LIFE IS NOT ALWAYS "ROSY." All people have struggled at some point in their lives and to some degree. What is fascinating about the human condition is that we continue to strive for something better. Look at history. If we hadn't done that, we would still be in the Stone Age! We innately desire to seek a better life for ourselves, be it through a job, a house, a family, or a situation. And Mike Flynn and his wife Julia are two people who are doing just that.

They had discussed moving to Florida as a joke for a while. The amenities in Tampa, Orlando, and Port Canaveral were enticing. Mike's work is in the hospitality industry and there would be plenty of work available as his stay-at-home-dad status was coming to an end soon. "The whole corridor is just loaded with amazing potential. It's crazy." And of course, the biggest feature was Walt Disney World.

A move to Florida now seemed plausible for the family. They were tired of the two-hour commute to shopping areas and they were "done" with the brutal winters of Michigan that they had experienced for the last five years.

Julia is a certified ophthalmology assistant. She started to apply for jobs in Florida during the spring of 2016, thinking that it would be August, perhaps September, before she would secure one in her field. But fate had something different in mind. Julia landed a job a couple of months later.

The family quickly prepared for the 1200-mile move. And in June 2016, they set off on their journey to a new life – a better life. Mike drove the truck with all their belongings while Julia followed behind in the car with their three children and their dog.

It was daunting to move that quickly. If anyone had told them in January that they would be moving to Florida that June, he would have thought that they were crazy, Mike said.

To visit the Magic Kingdom was not a part of the family's budget at this point. A one-day excursion for them would cost them nearly $500. They would have to wait. However, Mike soon discovered the Florida resident rates on passes and the option for a payment plan along with it. A trip to the parks seemed to be a possibility sooner than he had originally thought.

After taking a couple of months to settle in, Mike brought Julia and the kids to Disney Springs for a daytime outing. He had something up his sleeve...or in this case, in his pocket, and he was excited to share it. Mike gathered his family together and handed Julia and the children each a plastic temporary Walt Disney World annual pass. Julia looked at Mike. She is not one to cry very often but she did at this. They couldn't believe it! It was like Christmas for them. It was a very magical moment Mike remembers.

The family immediately drove over to the Magic Kingdom and caught the ferry over to the park. "It was going to be a quick trip but we just wanted to get us in there."

It was getting dark and the lights were glowing, adding to the beautiful sight when the family walked in for the very first time. It seemed very surreal to them. They walked slowly down Main Street USA to the castle. Julia was understandably quite emotional. Mike kept asking himself *Am I really here?*

He was trying to reconcile with the child in him who was raised by a single mother in London, Ontario, Canada. Walt Disney World had been for rich kids, he had been taught a long time before. His family would never be able to visit such a place. But he was there now. He was living in Florida, and he was now at Walt Disney World with his own family. It was beyond a hope and a dream to a young Mike Flynn.

Mike's mom had passed away in 2014 and he wished that she could have been a part of all of this with his family. "I think she would have been proud to see we are a part of that magic."

They continued to walk around the park, unsure of where they were going, taking in everything that they saw. Their first ride was It's A Small World as there was only a five-minute wait for the attraction.

The family got into the boat. Julia sat up front with two of the boys while Mike sat behind her with another. They held hands throughout the ride while tears silently rolled down Julia's cheeks. She never thought she would be at the Magic Kingdom that day, and this was not lost on her.

It was a beautiful experience for the family. "I could do it once a week [It's A Small World] every week and just love that."

He and their 7-year-old also rode the Astro Orbiter attraction at Tomorrowland that evening. Mike had gauged it to be about a 3 on a scale of 10 for fear. He was wrong. It was more like a 5 or 6, but his son loved it and turned to his dad and said, "That was the best ever!"

The family lives about seven miles from the parks. They can go into the park for the morning, come home for lunch, and return in the afternoon.

They have visited Animal Kingdom and loved the Kilimanjaro Safaris, especially when the tall, beautiful giraffe liked to follow them, Mike chuckled.

Some of Mike's most memorable times are doing the character meet-and-greets. The very first character they met was Mickey Mouse himself. And he spoke to them. "That just blew us out of the water. And that's when the inner kid in me just came out."

Julia laughed at him because he usually doesn't get choked up at things. "I just really like that it was an immersive experience," he said.

The kids are at the perfect age, and Mike and Julia are becoming like kids again too, going through those park gates.

At the time of this writing, Mike is preparing for his new role as a cast member with the Walt Disney company. It is this role that will finally fulfill this family's dream of a better life.

MS. INCREDIBLE

*"If I'm sad or stressed, Disneyland is my happy place.
I can go and recharge and then start all over again."*

— ANGELICA DORIA

WHEN I FIRST STARTED INTERVIEWING people, I thought I knew what kind of story I was going to get. After all, this was why I had invited people to be a part of this book. However, I found time and again that I would get more of a story than I initially thought I would, and this story is no exception. Occasionally, you meet someone who does things that are challenging to say the least. It usually entails one or even a couple of things that have our mouths dropping in awe. My next story is about a woman who absolutely blew me away with *everything* she does. And not only was she gracious about it, her infectious happy attitude was truly inspiring.

Angelica Doria is an only child who fell in love with Disney at a very early age. She started visiting Disneyland with her mom and dad when she was just a year old. Unfortunately, while she was a young girl, her parents got a divorce. Her mom continued to take Angelica, but things were just not the same for her. "My father has been out of the picture for a very long time." This is one of the reasons that Angelica returns to Disneyland over and over again: to remember her family when it was just the three of them together. "It always comes down to the memories, that is what keeps drawing me back. Sometimes I just go and sit on a bench and people watch. It brings back the memories of the things my family did together."

When Angelica was a little older, she relished the day she could start work and buy herself an annual pass so that she could go whenever she wanted. The years went by and Angelica joined the army. She served her country for eleven years and retired from the military in 2014. While in the army, Angelica had two sons; one is 9 years old now and has autism and her youngest is 4 years old, and has spina bifida. He was never supposed to be able to walk. To add to the challenging lot that she has been dealt in life, Angelica is a single parent. She also works full time as a financial analyst and goes to school, working towards her MBA. If this hasn't overwhelmed you, the last piece surely will. She is also a multi-marathoner, and trains several days a week. What an amazing woman!

"It's my kids who push me to do better – I want to be a good example – show them what Mom can do – especially when they grow up and know what it takes to get things accomplished." Because of the stressful life that she leads, Angelica turns to Disney for a reprieve. "If I'm sad or stressed, Disneyland is my happy place. I can go and recharge and then start all over again."

Now that Angelica is back home from her time in the military, she has been developing new friendships through several Disney Facebook groups that she belongs to. Apart from their mutual love of Disney, she has discovered that many of her Disney friends are runners too, and they compete in various marathons. Angelica used to like running. A lot. It was always a goal of hers to run a half-marathon one day. Being in the military, she had been used to running. "You had to run. You were not given a choice. I wanted to do a half-marathon just to say I did it, and that's it."

She had talked about it for years but she never really did anything about it. (Sound familiar, anyone?) However, after meeting some of the Disney runners, she decided to make it happen. *I actually have to do something about it instead of just saying it* she thought. And this is just how Angelica started running again. One of her friends, a fellow Disney marathoner, stepped in with some wise words for anyone wanting to do a Disney run. The friend wanted her to have a good experience with a Disney run and have time to stop and see the characters or do a ride. To attain that, it was suggested that Angelica do some local races and improve her time.

Angelica ran one of her first two 10K races in January 2016. And she was hooked. She started training three to four times a week indoors on a treadmill up to one and two hours at a time. She never gets to run outside until race day, which is very different from running on a treadmill. This enables Angelica to bring her children along with her to the child-care provided at the gym. Because she is on a treadmill, she just keeps pushing herself and will run up to 10 miles at a time.

Finally, the day arrived when she would compete in her first half-marathon at Disneyland. It was Labor Day week-end in September 2016. "When you finish your first half-marathon, no one can describe to you or tell you how you will feel after you finish. Once you cross the finish line, it gets pretty emotional," she says. And crossing the finish line after a full marathon "is a whole different story," which Angelica did the weekend after her first half. "The half-marathon was something I had always wanted to do but I did it mainly for my kids," she says.

Angelica has since completed the Avengers run in November 2016, the Dopey run at Walt Disney World with a couple of friends in January 2017, and the Star Wars at Disneyland in January 2017. She also signed up for the Dark Side marathon at Walt Disney World in April. "It's crazy – it's kind of hard to keep up with my schedule now," she laughs. (I can't imagine!)

In all of Angelica's accomplishments, it is what hap-pened the day before her first half-marathon at Disneyland in September 2016 that will forever be etched in her heart and mind. She remembers that morning well. She had just run the 10K, her very first Disney run earlier that day. But it was her youngest son's experience that she is the proudest of. Her 3-year-old son, the one with spina bifida who was never supposed to be able to walk, amazingly ran his first 100m race for kids! "It was really, really emotional that morning." Her son loves Disney as much as his mom now. "For him to see all the characters during the race, he was beyond excited. He was waving to everybody and it was just amazing to see that." There was a culmination of three wonderful things for Angelica that day; "my love for my kids, my love for running, and my love for Disney that came together for me."

This incredibly hardworking, determined, and inspiring mother of two – aka Ms. Incredible – was on top of the world that day.

SNOW WHITE'S GIFT

*"I get the magic of Disney and it makes
me feel good to spread that."*

— DISNEY DREAM GIRLS PODCASTER, MICHELLE YOUNG

I AM ALWAYS AMAZED AT how the wonderful and infectious spirit of Disney transfers to guests through other guests. It's like paying the magic forward, so to speak.

Michelle Young is a Disney fan extraordinaire. She has been as far back as she can remember. She loves Snow White and has a special affinity towards this princess. However, you wouldn't know it based on her first encounter with her in the form of the movie *Snow White and the Seven Dwarfs*. Her godmother was the one to take Michelle, her brother, and her cousins to see the movie at the cinema in England where they live. What was to be an enjoyable and memorable after-noon at the cinema turned out to be memorable all right.

She will never forget seeing *Snow White and the Seven Dwarfs* – her first Disney movie. Things were going along well until the old hag appeared on the screen, terrifying little Michelle. She started screaming at the top of her lungs – and she kept screaming. They all had to leave unfortunately, without seeing the rest of the movie. "I remember my cousins and brother absolutely hating me because they missed the end."

Michelle has visited, in chronological order, Walt Disney World, Disneyland, and Disneyland Paris, "which seems bizarre because the nearest one was actually the last one I went to." After being fortunate enough to bring her three children on a three-week holiday, Michelle "fell completely in love with the [Walt Disney World] theme park." And is now a regular visitor to the Disney parks.

She has met and made many friends through their mutual love of all things Disney. On one occasion, Michelle went to a Disney meet-up in the UK where she met a lady by the name of Kim (not me, by the way), who was starting up a Disney podcast. Michelle was supportive of the show, listening regularly and emailing questions. One day, she received a message from Kim inviting her to co-host a segment she was having on Snow White. "You're the person to speak to," Kim told her. Michelle loved the idea and discussed the history and evolution of the film on the show. From there, she was invited to become a part of the show. After working on about 50 shows together, Kim decided to retire. At this juncture, Michelle and a friend, a fan of the show, decided to start a new podcast called *Disney Dream Girls.* It's a wonderful podcast that celebrated its third anniversary in 2016.

Doing her podcasts has given Michelle opportunities to meet people from all over the world who have hosted her on many occasions. On a trip to Disneyland she was shown around and visited Walt's favourite restaurant, the Tam O' Shanter Inn (the ribs are divine, she said) near the Disney Studios in Burbank; Walt's final resting place where she was able to pay her respects; the Walt Disney Family Museum in San Francisco; and the Griffith Park carousel where it all began. "I feel very honoured through doing the podcasts to have met so many people who took me on these trips."

On one of her trips to Disneyland Paris, Michelle found out that the Disneyland hotel was going to be hosting a brunch with none other than Snow White. With her love for this princess, Michelle knew she just had to go. She is a school teacher and had to work both Friday and the following Monday. Her friend Peter, another podcaster, and his family were going to go, and Michelle was invited along. She drove the five hours to London after work to meet up with them and together they drove the seven hours to Paris after getting up at 4:00 on Saturday morning. She was looking forward to having brunch with Snow White after travelling so many hours to get there. The hotel offers brunch every Sunday. They begin with a glass of champagne and have seafood, carving stations and other amazing foods and desserts, Michelle shares.

On the morning of the brunch, the family and Michelle were bounding as characters. Michelle had gone as Snow

White, of course. She wore a blue dress, yellow leggings, a red belt, Mickey ears decorated with crystals that she had made, topped off with a Seven Dwarfs necklace. They were all set and very excited about this brunch, but they had started noticing on social media outlets that there was a slight possibility that there may be a change in the theme since it was Father's Day.

I don't know why; you would think that the fathers out there would appreciate Snow White too!

The group arrived at noon and in the back of their minds, they were preparing themselves for the possibility that it might not be the Snow White brunch they had been expecting. It was evident though that when they were ushered into the restaurant, everyone present *was* expecting a Snow White brunch. There were a lot of beautifully dressed princesses in Snow White attire in the room. They sat down and began chatting with a couple of families around them. The family nearby had two daughters: one who was 4 years old, and the other was a bit younger. The 4-year-old was dressed in a beautiful Snow White gown. Her parents had just bought the outfit the day before specifically for this brunch. She was so excited; she could hardly wait Michelle observed.

And then they started to see the characters coming out and they were all dressed as pirates. Michelle began to have a sick feeling in her stomach. Although it was neat to see them all dressed as pirates as Michelle had never seen them this way before, her heart sank a bit. This was not going to be a Snow White brunch after all. She was pretty disappointed because she had come all this way just to see Snow White. If she was disappointed, Michelle thought, she could only imagine how the children must have felt, especially the little girl she got to know sitting beside them. Michelle would get over it she knew; she would have another opportunity to see Snow White and the Seven Dwarfs on her upcoming trip to Walt Disney World.

She turned to the family when she heard the little girl's heart-wrenching cries. "I don't know what it was about it – it just sort of struck a chord with me." Perhaps it was because of her empathy as a mother or her own love for Snow White. At any rate, Michelle sprang into action. She wanted to do something to help ease this little girl's sorrow. She looked in her bag for stickers or glow sticks that she usually carried around with her to hand out to people in the parks. But this time, she was out of luck. She had not replenished her stash.

Michelle went to the little girl's dad and told him that she wanted to try something to help make his daughter happy again and confirmed that they would still be there when she had returned. With that, she promptly left the restaurant.

Down the corridor she went and quickly entered the gift shop. *I have got to find something Snow White and mend this little girl's broken heart*, she thought to herself. Thankfully she found a little pin with Snow White on it. She asked them to put it in a little Disney bag for her.

How am I going to give this to her without her parents thinking I'm weird? was Michelle's next thought. It was worth about 8 or 9 Euros, and she was worried that they might think she was a bit strange. *I'll have to put something together but in a magical Disney way so it doesn't sound sort of creepy.*

Then an idea was hatched.

Upon returning to the restaurant, Michelle made her way over to the little girl, who was cuddling with her father, still visibly upset.

"I've just been out of the restaurant and come back in again and Snow White asked can I give this to the little girl dressed up as her?" The little girl didn't respond, so her father took the bag from Michelle.

"She's given this to me and she's really sorry that she has not made the brunch today. One of the dwarfs is poorly. She'd knew you'd come and she wanted to give you this. Shhh," Michelle said. "Don't tell all the others here because they will be really upset."

Her father carefully opened the bag and exclaimed "Look what it is!" The little girl saw that it was a beautiful Snow White pin. She became very excited while her mother pinned it to her gown. "Seeing her happy was like someone had given *me* a gold bar because it made *me* so happy. I was nearly in tears," Michelle says.

The little girl's mom spoke with Michelle after and told her how kind it was of her to do something like this for her daughter. They were going home the next day and no one had ever done anything like that for them before. Michelle explained to the mom that she is a Disney fan and she likes to do nice things for people. "I get the magic of Disney and it makes me feel good to spread that."

As parents, we want to make sure everything is okay for our children, especially on a trip to Disney. We can't always make our children's hurts better. And it is particularly heartbreaking for parents when we are helpless to do that.

I know that Michelle made that little girl's day, but I think she made the parents' day even more because she, a perfect stranger, helped heal their daughter's broken heart when they couldn't, themselves. I think about the kindness behind Snow White's gift that day and the many other times that Michelle has given out stickers and glow sticks to the children she encounters. And it just warms my heart.

"I know when I've had little things done for me at Disney and how it made me feel," Michelle shared.

I don't know about you, but I am going to remember the next time I go to Walt Disney World to bring some glow sticks and stickers for my family to give out to others, too.

"It's just sharing around the Disney magic."

THANK YOU

*"I will never, ever forget this kindness
and compassion shown to me."*

— KIMBERLEY BOUCHARD

I HAVE BEEN WAITING NEARLY eight years now for the opportunity to thank the cast members who helped me and my family through our darkest hours aboard our very first Disney cruise. The compassion and thoughtfulness shown to us are difficult to put into words. But I will try; it is time.

Our family of five along with my parents had cruised a couple of times, but it had never been on a Disney cruise before. We were so excited that we could afford it if we went during the off-season in September. This was a dream come true for us Disney fans.

Our family of five would be driving from Alberta, Canada, at that time in our motor home, stopping at Walt

Disney World for a long-awaited visit, then carry on to our cruise. My parents would frequently join us on our visits, but they were not able to do so this time. On one occasion when we were on our way to the airport, we stopped to say goodbye to Grandma and Grandpa. Our children are close to their grandparents and would not be seeing them for a couple of weeks. All of a sudden, my mom and dad hopped in, much to the surprise and delight of our children. Their beloved grandparents were coming to Walt Disney World too!

We had many great times together. I fondly remember the time that my dad wore his pirate hat with dreadlocks attached at the Pirate and Princess party to match his grandsons'. Another great party we attended was Mickey's Merry Christmas Party. It was so cold that we all bought warm Disney hats to wear in the park. My sons, my husband, Jacques, and my dad wore various light-up Sorcerer Mickey and Goofy Christmas hats. We were quite a sight, the seven of us, and we lit up the night.

Mom and Dad were good sports about it all. They were always up for some wonderful adventures with us whenever we would get back to Walt Disney World. Their sense of humour and good nature would stay intact while they went everywhere around the parks that we thought would be fun.

Our uncertainty of even embarking on such a journey that September was in question. My dad, Florian, was dying of brain cancer. It was a horrific 15-month battle of a young healthy man who was only 69 years old. Although he was sleeping more, Dad was still up and about in the house with assistance.

We were advised by the doctors and my mom to go on our vacation. Dad would be okay. With conflicting emotions, we began our four-day journey of 4500 kilometers (2800 miles) to Walt Disney World. I called home frequently talking with both my parents, especially with my dad. It was deceptive though, because my dad sounded like his old self on the phone. It helped my aching heart, pretending that he wasn't even ill at all.

We had a wonderful visit at Walt Disney World despite what was weighing heavily on our hearts. It was a reprieve from the emotional journey we had been on for the last 15 months since we had received my dad's diagnosis. We were lighthearted the day that we headed to Port Canaveral for our 7-night cruise aboard the *Disney Magic*. It was September 6, 2009.

It was like experiencing Disney for the first time again. We could not believe our eyes. It was Disney, but on a ship! The greeting by name of each family was a wonderful welcome. The magic of *The Magic* was putting us under her spell.

As everyone does after they board, we hit the dining area first. It was lunch time and we were hungry. We could not believe the beautiful buffet waiting for us with everything imaginable to eat. It was as stunning to look at as it was delicious to eat. The smiling cast members serving us behind the food counters and bussing our tables added to the friendly atmosphere.

The next thing everyone typically does, is explore the ship. We checked out the kids' programs and registered our children who were 13, 11, and 9 years old at the time.

Our room became available and we set out to locate it. It was a beautiful room with a view off the balcony. We decided that the children would only be allowed out on the balcony if they were accompanied by Mommy or Papa. That was no problem at all for them. The height of our room and the water below was enough of a deterrent for our kids. We were lucky; our kids were good about listening to their parents.

A trip to the pool and a wonderful dinner and show topped that most amazing day. A call home earlier that day assured me that things were fine with Dad as well.

Our first stop was at Key West, Florida on Monday, September 7. It was hard to believe that this place was still attached to the mainland. We explored the town and bought some Kino sandals that Key West is known for. The shop was a little place with a small counter up front and the warehouse where they made the sandals behind it. There were a lot of varieties of sandals with great prices too. Another phone call that evening before heading out to sea assured me that things were still all right at home. However, things were not quite the way they seemed, but I didn't find this out until later.

The cast members working in the dining area were exceptional; they were on point every single time. We had two children with severe nut allergies and they accommodated that Disney style. In this case, they let the children choose from the menu the night before so that the chefs could take extra precaution in handling their food. They even had spe-cial desserts waiting for them in the refrigerator throughout the day. They just needed to ask a cast member in dining to retrieve it for them. The service was outstanding; the genu-ine caring of the cast members was incredible.

The ship was small enough to be able to walk from bow to stern without it being too much of a chore. With a smaller ship, you also have a smaller population. The cast members began remembering our names in the places that we would frequent. Some of them working in the gift shops even re-membered our room number!

On Tuesday, September 8, we had a port of call in Mexico. I hurried off the ship to make a call come from a payphone. Things had changed a bit; I could hear it in my mom's voice. I spoke with my dad briefly telling him that we would be heading straight home after we disembarked and that I loved him. When I hung up the phone, worry began seeping in. The port of call the next day had me running off the ship to phone home and check on my dad. I would always call twice; once when we first disembarked and then again before we boarded the ship. Sometimes I was able to talk to him; other times my dad would be resting.

I tried to hide my worry from the kids, and each night we would pray for my dad and pray that we could get home to see him on time. When we were at sea, I made a call home from our stateroom. Anybody who has made a ship-to-shore call will know that they are expensive. A 10-minute call back to Canada cost $150 USD.

I was distraught. I pulled myself together as best as I could and headed down to Guest Services. I asked the cast member if there was another way that I could call home that would not cost quite so much. I explained the situation as best as I could. It was all I could do to not start sobbing in her arms. The cast member returned after speaking to someone a few moments later. She asked me what the number was. And then she told me...and I will **never, ever forget** this kindness and compassion shown to me. She told me that anytime that I needed to call home, they would make the call home for me, at no charge.

I couldn't believe it. I don't know where I got the strength to thank her without completely losing it. She dialed home immediately and moved the phone to the corner of the counter to give me some privacy. Each time that I would make a call, I would try and make sure that there were no other guests around. I needed not only emotional space, but I needed physical space as well. I didn't want to ruin someone's vacation if I happened to start crying on the phone.

I remained in the room that evening. Jacques took the kids to dinner to help me collect myself. I just wanted to be alone. I went out to sit on the balcony, lost in my thoughts. It was soothing to see the moon on the ocean, which appeared to be made of glass, it was so calm. I was thinking about how this ocean and moon were here long before we were and would continue to be there long after we were gone. And I thought about the days to come. And I cried.

My husband returned with a takeout dinner from the dining room and checked in on me before taking the children to the evening show.

The next day, September 11, would be our last full day aboard the ship. We disembarked on Castaway Cay, Disney's private island in the Caribbean. I couldn't call home yet because of the time zone. I didn't feel right about calling at 5 a.m.

That day, our first on Castaway Cay, was absolutely amazing. That island is our family's favourite port of call now, hands down. We walked off the ship and there, waiting off to the side of the walkway, was my favourite pirate, Captain Jack Sparrow. I was wearing a pin that my family had bought for me. It had a heart with the words "I love Jack Sparrow" on it. I stood beside Captain Sparrow laughing my head off. He had leaned over to read the pin and responded, "I love me too!" It felt good to laugh.

We had a wonderful day at the beach resting and swimming and enjoying the beautiful island. The barbeque the cast members had set up for us was delicious. The kids also enjoyed the self-serve banana ice cream that they had been eating on the ship.

At about 3 p.m. my anxiety level started to rise, and I wanted to call home. I went off searching for a telephone with no luck. I stopped to speak with a cast member who was in a little information booth set up along the walkway. When I inquired if there was a phone on the island that I could use, she apologized that unfortunately there wasn't.

She asked me right away if I was the woman whose father was…she didn't complete her sentence. She didn't have to by the look on my face.

I couldn't believe that she would know about this. I was one of thousands on that beach. Somehow news had circulated on the ship that my dad was dying. We had known by that time that we needed to get home immediately after we disembarked. The cast members offered to escort us off the ship so that we could be on our way home as quickly as possible.

We went back on board the ship, and I went directly to Guest Services while my husband brought the kids back to the stateroom. The cast member dialled my number as soon as she saw me and handed me the phone.

I thought I had time. Although I knew that time was running out, I thought I would still see my dad again. It was at that moment though that I knew that we were not going to make it home. Dad had not woken up; he was in transition, heading to his new heavenly life.

I hung up the phone and ran to the elevator. I didn't want to ruin someone's day by losing it, and I was especially worried about all the children around. I was in major distress; I had to get to our stateroom fast. I got back to the room and the look on my face said it all to my family.

And so, we waited. The news came less than three hours later through an email from my sister-in-law. There was no other way to reach us she apologized. I called home immediately to speak briefly with my mom. That was the darkest and most difficult night of my life - of our lives.

I'm sure people were wondering what was going on hearing our heart-wrenching cries as they passed by our state room that night.

As promised, we were escorted off the ship early the next morning. While waiting for the all clear to disembark, the cast members kept us out of sight of the public for both our privacy and self preservation. The measures taken to help our family through this time were exceptional.

I would like to take the opportunity to thank every cast member on *The Magic* who helped our family cope with the most difficult of circumstances, that my family faced from the moment we boarded to the moment we disembarked and everything in-between.

You cast members are a class act.

Thank you.

DISNEY SISTERS

"We all have that special connection with people that love Disney. I am closer to these girls than any of my childhood friends. We are inseparable. Nothing ever seems like it has changed when we get together."

— *JENNIFER BALDOVINOS*

ONE THING THAT I HAVE often been puzzled about is how, in rooms filled with people, you meet certain ones that then become your friends? It happens over and over again and it can happen at any given point in time. Being there at the right place at the right time – is it serendipity? Luck? Destiny? Or something else entirely?

I still don't know the answer, but what I do know is that often people will come into your life at precisely the right time. The next story is about just that. Instead of meeting one or even two others, these *four* young women met for the first time in a room filled with people, and amazingly, became lifelong friends.

Jennifer Baldovinos has always had a love for Disney and even had the opportunity to visit Disneyland a few times when she was younger. When Jennifer's older sister told her about the opportunities available for her through a college program at Walt Disney World, she decided to check it out. After interviewing for a merchandising position with her retail experience, she was accepted into the program and headed to Florida in August of 2002.

When Jennifer arrived at the Orlando airport, she was fortunate enough to have a friend living nearby who offered to pick her up and drop her off at Walt Disney World to check in as a new cast member. Jennifer remembers that day, nearly 16 years ago now, as if it were yesterday.

All new cast members checking in were asked to leave their driver's licenses temporarily on a nearby table. As she put hers down, Jennifer homed in on another Colorado license near hers. *Someone from home* she thought. She immediately turned to the girl behind her as they were placed in another line and asked if she was the one from Colorado. Affirming that she was, the girls immediately struck up a conversation. While they were chatting, they realized that from the allocation of all the people in line, that they were going to be roommates.

Jennifer and her new roommate, Beth, were to live in Apartment 5303 at Walt Disney World. Turning to the girls behind them, they asked if they were assigned to 5303 as well.

An affirmative answer came from them and right away the four of them "hit it off," Jennifer said. Joining Jennifer and Beth was Angela from New Orleans, who was on her second college program, and Ellen, who was from New Jersey.

The first night they were there, the girls all went to the Magic Kingdom. Angela had worked there during her previous college program so she was able to take the others backstage behind the scenes. "We were in awe of everything. It was all of our first time in the tunnels," Jennifer shares. After the Magic Kingdom, they headed off to Epcot where they got a picture of the four of them in front of the Epcot ball. "We put little yellow flowers in our hair and thought it was just great." The photograph in front of the ball would prove to be a pivotal moment in the girls' lives.

Jennifer was assigned to what was known as the Gourmet Pantry at the time, which incorporated a deli, candy store, and housewares, and is now the Earl of Sandwich at Disney Springs. Beth was placed in merchandise at Liberty Square in the Magic Kingdom, and Ellen worked in food and beverage at Pinocchio's in the Magic Kingdom. Angela worked at the Tower of Terror as a bellhop.

Despite having a different schedule from her three roommates (they would be finishing their shifts at 6 p.m. while Jennifer would be starting hers), Angela, Beth, and Ellen would all stop by to say hello. "We would always try to visit each other at work. We'd go a few minutes before someone was off so we could just meet up afterwards and go play," Jennifer says. The girls would spend all their days off together. "We were inseparable the whole internship. We would do fun things at night, take pictures, and buy souvenir pins from the parks." Three of the girls were Catholic and would go to mass together as well. "It was crazy how much we had in common."

One of the biggest things to happen to the girls during their program at Walt Disney World was 9/11. They were all away from their families, and Ellen's dad worked in the World Trade Center. Back then, there were not many cell phones at the time. The worry, the consoling of their friend and then finally getting through to him and finding out he was okay stands out significantly. Their support for each other through the best of times and the worst of times further cemented their friendship.

After their programs were finished, their friendship continued to grow. They would see each other two to three times a year and go back to Walt Disney World every other year. When each of them got engaged, they were there, hosting bridal showers for each other. They were all bridesmaids at each other's weddings, too. They threw baby showers for each other as their children were born. To celebrate their 5th friendship anniversary, the girls went to Chicago where Beth had just had a baby. As long as they were together, that was all that mattered.

As their lives got busier, the girls remained in touch. Apart from meeting up, they would frequently email or text each other with a quick message of "thinking about you, love you." No matter how busy they get, they make the effort to stay connected and make sure that they are all still talking with each other regularly.

On their 15th anniversary in August of 2016, they all met up in Orlando, where Ellen still lived. She had just had a baby and rather than have her take him out in the heat, the girls hung out together at Ellen's home. They knew that they had to visit one park, and they chose Epcot. They wanted to recreate the picture of themselves lined up in front of the Epcot ball. They did all the fun girly things, too. They got manicures and pedicures and they went out for dinner. All of them enjoy scrapbooking so they would sit around and reminisce about old times. "We have constantly stayed in touch. I am closer to these girls than any of my childhood friends. We are inseparable. Nothing ever seems like it has changed when we get together. We all have that special connection with people that love Disney."

And who was to know that nearly 16 years ago, this connection would spark a wonderful friendship with these four women that I call Disney sisters.

It's pretty amazing when you think about it – all the new cast members getting into line that day meeting and checking in. It could have been a variety of combinations of people, really. Serendipity? Luck? Destiny?

Perhaps it was a little pixie dust…

P.S. Jennifer is married with three children and lives in Colorado. She does administrative work for sales and training for a medical device company there. Beth lives in

Chicago where she is a school science teacher. Angela lives in Louisiana with her husband and young son. She works in financing at Chase Bank. Ellen lives in Orlando with her husband and baby boy. She works for the Disney Vacation Club.

THE COLLECTOR

*"I don't know very many people in my circles
who are what I'd call Disney nuts like I am"*

— DAN HARTLEY

DAN HARTLEY HAD BEEN A part of Walt Disney World from its
inception; but he didn't know it at the time. His father, a
plumber, was one of the hundreds that helped to build the
Magic Kingdom, which was the very first park at Walt Disney
World, from the ground up. He helped lay the piping and
assisted in plumbing the many different areas that required
water at the park.

Dan remembers going to the periphery of the worksite
and seeing construction trucks and a lot of dirt. He saw
lots of people wearing white hard hats with a little Mickey
Mouse on them, which he thought was pretty cool. "But
still, even at that time, it didn't register with me what was

going on. I didn't understand what Disney was. I was pretty young."

This would serve as the very beginning of his collection of memories of Walt Disney World.

At some time during the construction phase, his dad brought their family to what was called *The Mickey Mouse Review*. Dan's family, along with other families, were ushered into a large room with railings to lean against – like the 360-degree theatre at the Canadian Pavilion at Epcot. There were ladies at the front wearing smart uniforms and little hats like the stewardesses back in the day Dan shares. They were doing a slide presentation about what Walt Disney World would look like when it was finished. "It didn't quite affect me yet; I didn't realize what I was looking at."

Disney was very secretive about their Florida project. They used a variety of business names to purchase the land that now comprises Walt Disney World. Some of these names can be seen on the upper story windows of a building on the right hand side of Main Street USA near the Crystal Arts shop.

It was a reporter for the *Sentinel Star*, now called *The Orlando Sentinel*, by the name of Emily Bavar who finally broke the news. She was poking around and noticed hundreds of thousands of acres of swamp land being bought up in central Florida.

The year was 1965 and Disneyland was celebrating its 10th anniversary, affectionally named the "Tencennial." Reporters were flown in from across the United States to be entertained for this event in exchange for covering it. One of these reporters was Emily. She was instructed by her boss to ask whether Disney was planning on building a theme park in Florida. Emily approached Disney's publicist, a man named Charles Ridgeway, and asked about it. He didn't know anything about it (he actually didn't) and suggested that she ask Walt himself at the luncheon the next day. When Emily confronted Walt, he looked shocked that she would know. Things snowballed from there and Disney was forced into making an early announcement. Walt and Roy Disney and then Governor Haydon Burns, held a press conference on November 15, 1965, confirming their purchase of 47 square miles (120 square kilometers) of land.

And the rest, as they say, is history.

Dan returned with his family for his first visit to Walt Disney World in 1977 when he was 11 years old. "There was an entrance fee and then you purchased A, B, C, D, and E tickets. The E tickets were the best ones, for rides like Space Mountain. I rode it with my mom, who was terrified the whole time. We had a great time," he chuckles.

The 20,000 Leagues Under the Sea attraction was there as were the Gondolas and the Race Cars. The Race Cars were a big deal to Dan, because you were given a driver's licence with one of the characters on it before you drove your car. He remembers seeing several of the licences on the seats in the car and took them home with him. These I believe, would be the beginning of Dan's Disney collection.

In addition to the licences, they bought a 3'x3' map of the Magic Kingdom that day. Dan still has it forty years later. "It is one of my most prized possessions." Dan's dad made him a Robin Hood style hat and embroidered his name on it for the trip. He still has the hat as well. "It was kind of cool for me and started my love for Disney. I was hooked from that moment on."

His next trip wasn't until 1980 when Dan went with his high school choir. They were a part of the one thousand member choir performing at Christmas time that year. "It was a phenomenal trip with phenomenal memories."

Dan has been to Walt Disney World approximately two hundred times. He even spent a summer there as a cast member working at Big Thunder Mountain Railroad where he collected even more memories.

Dan has also continued collecting Disney pieces. "I have a lot of older things and I have some new things too – a mix of a lot of things together." His collection has approximately seven hundred different items in it now, he shares. Dan's Disney casting ID and casting badge are especially dear to his heart. He has an 8-inch plastic Donald Duck from around 1971 and a Mickey Mouse gumball machine from the 1950's in his collection that he is fond of too.

One day when his daughter was coming home from work, she spotted the robot Wall-E just sitting out beside a garbage can. Knowing that her dad would appreciate it, she picked it up and brought it home. "I couldn't believe that someone would *do* that," Dan said. When his daughter gave it to him, it let out its signature '*Waaallleee*' voice. It was a wonderful addition to his collection.

Dan finds his Disney pieces mostly at thrift stores. He collects them because he loves Disney so much. Each item he finds has a special meaning for him. Each one is a part of his love for Disney and how it is representative of his life. Disney is his happy place where he can lose himself. Disney allows Dan to remake memories at the most wonderful place on earth.

For Dan, Disney is a collection of happiness, both new and old, tangible and intangible.

MISADVENTURE

"If it was going to happen anywhere, let it happen there."

— AMY YAVENUE WYAND

I LEARN SOMETHING NEW EVERY day, I often say to people. And when I receive a story, I tend to learn many new things. I love to hear about other people's adventures with Disney and share a few of my own. I think that most of us who love Disney do, too. Even though I have been to Walt Disney World too many times to count, I find that the more I learn about Disney, the more I realize that I don't know.

I was delighted to learn some new things from Amy Wyand while interviewing her about a particular vacation her family took during the summer of 2016. In this day and age of planning a Disney vacation– the flights, the hotel, the fast passes down to the dining times – sometimes life will step in and make you come to a halt – even while you are at Walt Disney World.

Amy has been a regular to Walt Disney World and says that since she was the only girl in the family with two brothers seven years and nine years older than she was, her mom would often take her to the park. After a few years, her brothers joined Amy and her mom on their Disney vacation. She had been to the park approximately eight times before she had children and has been bout fifteen times since.

Amy and her husband John, spent their honeymoon at Walt Disney World and stayed at the Polynesian resort. They combined their stay with a Disney cruise on what was known at the time as the Big Red Boat. It was the pre-Disney cruise line era.

As a multiple Disney cruiser, I had never heard of this boat before and was intrigued to learn more about it.

The Big Red Boat, as it was affectionately known, was a boat named the *Oceanic* owned by a now defunct company called Premier. The hull was painted red to look more unique, fun, and attractive to families, hence the name. It did 3-4 day sailings out of Port Canaveral to the Bahamas. There were Disney characters aboard that would mingle with the guests. It was pretty small compared to the fleet that the Disney Cruise Line has today.

Amy and her family have stayed at nearly every resort hotel at Walt Disney World. Each time they visit, they book not one, but two resort hotels to have two different resort experiences.

That sounds like a great idea if you don't mind packing up your things. And Disney is wonderful about transferring all your luggage for you to your new resort too, I might add.

Amy loves to plan vacations. She will never forget the vacation that she planned for her family in 2001 with her parents, brothers, and her own family that had grown to 4. They stayed at Fort Wilderness Lodge and the Beach Club to give them all a taste of both resorts. "It was so much fun," she remembers.

Amy's brother, who is nine years older, has a prosthetic leg. When they got off Space Mountain, he proclaimed "You know, I think I nearly lost my leg!" And laughed.

"It was a happy place because everyone was there," Amy said.

A new vacation was booked for her family for July 2016. They were really excited to be going. Amy had booked Old Key West for the first three nights, and the Yacht and Beach Club for the final five nights. Both are beautiful resorts, with the Beach Club boasting a three-acre sand-bottom pool, with a pirate ship water slide.

I love the Beach Club for its proximity to Epcot and Hollywood Studios. You can take about a ten minute walk to the backside of Epcot and take a short boat ride to Hollywood Studios as well.

The plan for Amy's family was to rent a car to meet up with friends on the day that they would be moving resorts. But life had other plans for them.

The family arrived on Monday, July 18, and they took the time to settle into Old Key West. Their son Matt, who had just turned 17, admitted that he wasn't feeling very well. Amy assured him that they weren't going to do much that day.

They would just be going to the restaurant to eat and then relax afterwards. They were slated to go to Animal Kingdom the next day.

It was really hot that day and Matt was sweating so profusely that he soaked right through his shirt. After riding Kilimanjaro Safaris, they realized something was not right. They went to First Aid and asked if Matt could lie down for a bit. He fell asleep soon after. While Amy sat with her son, John and their daughter Ellen, went off to ride Expedition Everest. Amy thought that Matt merely had a touch of the flu. They headed back to the room when Matt woke up and went out to eat. He seemed fine.

The next day was Wednesday, and they headed to Magic Kingdom. Matt went on the rides and appeared fine, although he was really walking slowly. He felt ill again later in the day, and again they thought that he had a touch of the flu.

On Thursday, they were changing resorts, but Matt was feeling so poorly that he asked to be taken to Urgent Care, a walk in medical clinic near Disney Springs. The clinic still had all of Matt's information for an ear infection from a few years prior. The doctor came in and took one look at Matt and told them, "You need to go to the hospital."

They had no idea what was going on and brought Matt to the nearby hospital. And things took a turn for the worse. They were in the ER for nearly eight hours, and his temperature went up to 103.5. On top of this, Matt had a reaction to some medication they had given him, developing a rapid heartbeat and the shakes. Because he was only 17 years old, they needed to get him to the Children's Hospital. However, they needed to stabilize him in order for the ambulance to transfer him.

They still did not know what was wrong at this point. Amy will never forget the stress of that day. Her son was in the hospital away from home, she had to deal with a hotel change, their luggage was in storage, the car needed to be renewed, and reservations needed to be cancelled.

Matt was finally able to be moved. Amy rode with him in the ambulance, while John and Ellen followed in the car. They arrived at the Florida Children's Hospital. "It was beautiful. The lobby was all Disney. You knew you were in Orlando. There were characters from the *Jungle Book* on the wall and they had cartoons playing. It was nice; it was impressive."

Security was like no other place they had been before. Photos were taken and driver's licenses were recorded before they were allowed to enter the hospital. There was even a phone located outside of the elevators that you needed to speak into before you could enter the elevator. "We had never experienced anything like that before. It was like they wanted to know where we were going, what our names were, and who we were going to see before they would allow the door to be opened."

It was around 10p.m. when they finally received the diagnosis. They had found a red and swollen appendix, and they were told that Matt would most likely need an appendectomy. He was booked for surgery the next morning at 11:30. It was not lost on Amy, that her oldest brother, the one who nearly "lost his leg" on the ride at Space Mountain on their trip in 2001, had passed away ten years earlier from a ruptured appendix.

John stayed with Matt at the hospital while Amy and Ellen went back to the hotel to sort things out. There was a lot that had to be dealt with and Amy's emotions were running understandably high. "It just wasn't the way it was supposed to be." And she had to keep explaining things repeatedly when speaking with all the different people she needed to speak with. Amy was exhausted and it was after midnight before she could finally go to sleep. But the folks at Disney took good care of them, making things as easy as possible for the family.

The security process was repeated when they returned to the hospital on Friday morning before Matt's surgery. Unknown to Amy and Ellen, they would soon encounter the unexpected from "a long time ago in a galaxy far, far, away."

It was very quiet on the hospital wing, and Amy and Ellen walked quickly and quietly towards Matt's room when they were completely taken by surprise. There, standing in front of them all along the hallway were Storm Troopers, and the Dark One himself, Darth Vader! They couldn't believe their eyes! They hadn't heard them at all, which added to their shock of seeing them all there. And *they were* a sight to be seen.

The Disney ambassador tending to Darth Vader and his cohorts asked if Amy was there to visit someone. Amy explained that yes, they were, and her son was just about to have surgery.

She wondered if Matt would like them to visit him. The woman assured Amy that Darth Vader and the Storm Troopers would not go into his room if he didn't want them to. They would stay out in the hall and wave to him from the doorway.

Amy went along to tell Matt about their encounter in the hall and asked him if he would be interested in seeing them for a quick visit. "Mom, I don't think so," Matt replied. He just didn't feel up to it and he was nervous about his surgery.

As promised, they remained in the hall outside his room and waved at Matt from the doorway. Matt smiled, thrilled that Storm Troopers and Darth Vader were just outside his hospital room. He turned to his family and said, "You know you're in Disney when they do *that*." They took a lot of pictures of the characters from his room. "I wanted them in the room," Amy confessed, but they wanted to respect their son's wishes.

The Storm Troopers and Darth Vader continued their journey down the hall to every single room. They asked the parents first if it was okay to enter their child's room. They were very respectful, Amy said. She could see them go all the way to the end of the hall; the rooms that they did not enter, they merely waved and then moved on. "It was just a class act."

Matt's surgery went well. Later that day, a woman came around with a puppy who did tricks to help cheer the patients (and the parents) up. She told them that she got the puppy specifically to put smiles on people's faces. Amy assured her that she really had for them.

The nurse that had tended to Matt from 7 a.m. to 9 p.m. that day really went out of her way to care for Matt and his family. The Wyand family lives close to the world-famous Albanese candy company. Amy had brought a few packages of their famous gummies along with them to give away on their vacation. Amy gave one to Matt's nurse, who was so kind and caring. The nurse of course, was not expecting to receive anything.

They never do, but they sure give a lot. What a nice way to show some gratitude, and you don't have to be in a Disney hospital to be able to do so either.

John turned to Amy later that day and said, "You know, you really made her day."

Matt was discharged Saturday afternoon with medication and post-surgery care instructions. The doctor had told them to "play it by ear" and to take their time right now. Matt took a nap at the hotel and they went out for dinner.

On Sunday, Matt was feeling a little bit better and managed to rest on an inner tube in the lazy river at the resort. It was a great second option for someone who was not allowed to swim or soak in a pool. After getting some more sleep, the family managed a couple of more days in the parks, taking it very slowly.

The family made the best of their misadventure. "If it was going to happen anywhere, let it happen there," Amy said.

And they will be back again. "Because this is our place," Amy said. Misadventure or not – it has, and always will have, a special place in their hearts.

THE DISNEY CONNECTION

"If this small group can do it – all of us cast members,
guests, from the CEO to a little child, why can't the
world pick up on it? It has been proven – humans
CAN [get along] in that 46 square miles."

— FATHER GEORGE GULASH

LIKE MANY OF US OF a certain age, George Gulash grew up watching the *Wonderful World of Disney – World of Color* on Sunday nights. A trip to a Disney park just wasn't in the foreseeable future for a variety of reasons. So instead, he lived the magic of Disney through television, movies, books, vinyl records, and games until he was able to experience it live for himself in a Disney park.

The far-reaching Disney magic touches the masses in as many ways as the diversity of the people themselves. You can only imagine my surprise and delight to meet Fr. George, a fellow Disney lover and Catholic priest that I now call a friend. Although you will find him in Disney t-shirts and various head attire, he does not hide the fact that he is a Catholic priest who enjoys Disney just as much as the next guy – and sometimes even more so. It is such a diverse community: Jewish, atheist, agnostic; every belief under the sun, every walk of life and Disney is what unites us, he says.

George grew up in a little coal mining town in Windber, Pennsylvania, where the rare big vacation was going to visit his aunt. A Disney park to little George existed somewhere "out there" in a place called California, which might as well have been on Mars. "It just wasn't going to happen," he explains. He has fond memories of watching Winnie the Pooh on the *Wonderful World of Disney*. This would mean that the kids had to shower and get their pajamas on early, and then they could all gather around the family television and watch. "I remember seeing Sleeping Beauty Castle with Tinkerbell and thinking, *WOW!*"

George grew up and received his calling to the priesthood. While studying at the Pontifical College Josephinum in Columbus, Ohio, a Disney store opened in a nearby mall. "I had never heard of a Disney store," Fr. George tells me. They were just starting up at the time. Walking around in the store, George noticed a 2-foot plush Winnie the Pooh. All his wonderful memories of his childhood on Sunday nights came flooding back. He bought it and it remained in his dorm room throughout college and seminary school. It was a daily, happy reminder of his childhood.

A friend he had studied with at the seminary was assigned to a parish in Daytona Beach, Florida. During a break, Fr. George decided to visit Fr. Peter, who told him that while he was visiting, they would go to Walt Disney World.

However, Fr. George declined. "Oh, I don't like amusement parks, I don't do rides, I don't like rollercoasters." His friend admonished him and said, "You aren't going all the way back to Pennsylvania to say you were in Florida and *NOT* go to Disney World!" Fr. George relented and agreed to go, but for one day only.

They arrived during Walt Disney World's 25th anniversary celebration when Fr. George was 34 years old. It wasn't until the Spectro Magic parade that he became a believer – a believer in the Disney magic. He and Fr. Peter stood on the corner of Town Square by Goofy's Candy Company as the parade was going by.

"I remember watching these floats, and I was just mesmerized."

Fr. Peter leaned over and asked Fr. George, "So what do you think?" Without taking his eyes off the parade, he told his friend, "it is absolutely magical." (I must mention here that until I started writing Fr. George's story, I hadn't thought about the parallel between St. Peter at the pearly gates of Heaven and Fr. Peter "opening the gates" to Walt Disney World.)

And that was it. He was hooked. The following year when Fr. George went down to visit again, it was he who convinced Fr. Peter that it was time for another visit to Walt Disney World. After all, he didn't want to go all the way back to Pennsylvania after saying he was in Florida and *not* go to Walt Disney World...

When Fr. Peter got assigned to a different parish, Fr. George realized that he *could* still visit Walt Disney World even if he had to do it on his own.

So that's exactly what he did. Fr. George would go down by himself. "I was quite okay with that." Eventually however, friends would ask to go along with him. He even took his mother, his sister, and her family along with him a few times.

In 2005, Fr. George made it to the original Disney park, Disneyland, for the 50th anniversary celebration. He remembers that day well, particularly while standing in the Plaza between California Adventure and Disneyland. He was staring at the train station and thought to himself *I have seen this so many times on TV and now I'm here!* He got quite choked up and decided to give his mother a call. Alarmed with how her son sounded, she asked him what was the matter. "Are you okay?" she asked.

"Mom" he replied, "I'm here! This is where Walt actually walked!" After being accompanied to Walt Disney World many times by friends, Fr. George felt he needed to also go on his own "to reclaim a bit of his first experiences." His love for Walt Disney World continues to grow and he is now up to visiting 25 days a year that he saves up for. Walt Disney World is his way of recharging. "I need to take care of me," he says in order to take care of the 600 families of his parish. And this year, in 2017, Fr. George will be celebrating his 25th anniversary to the priesthood!

Fr. George has learned a lot from Disney's "art of hospitality" that he applies to his parish ministry. "Walt Disney was a story teller and we tell our story as followers of Jesus. Disney uses sights, sounds, smells, and textures to bring you into the story. The Catholic Church does this as well in its sacramental system." Fr. George describes it in this light: "we smell the incense, we hear the bells, we taste the bread and wine, we kiss an icon, we shake hands, and we communicate. It's very physical to bring people into the story. You need to *experience* it and isn't that what draws us back to Disney?" He asks.

He tells his parish council that they can learn a lot from Disney because they are "past excellent in their marketing. Marketing is what we call *evangelization*." Why is it that anybody who knows Disney goes on talking about it forever? Fr. George asks. "It's because we believe in it, we have experienced it, and we want to share it." And that's why he wants to tell people that when we experience Jesus, isn't that something *we* want to share?

Fr. George tries to instill a sense of belonging within his parish. "We welcome people and make them feel important because they are. Without the people, there is no church. Without the people, there is no Disney. You know what the real magic is?" he asks me. "It's human kindness."

When visiting the parks, Fr. George always looks at the name tags of the cast members. If they are wearing a blue tag with white lettering, he congratulates them. The blue tag represents the Disney Legacy Award that is bestowed upon cast members by fellow cast members and supervisors in recognition for consistently honouring and demonstrating the Disney Dream.

After the recent passing of his mother, Fr. George went to Walt Disney World to grieve and heal. "It's my comfort zone." His first park and the last park that he visits is the Magic Kingdom. The train is always Fr. George's first ride of the day. On that trip, sitting quietly at the first stop at Frontierland, Fr. George was looking off to the left in the woods, lost in thought. He habitually would call his mom each morning to talk with her and see how she was doing. Sitting there, he realized that there would be no more calls; *well things are different now* he thought to himself. A cheerful "good morning" brought him out of his thoughts. He turned and saw a cast member standing there greeting him. Fr. George responded with a quick good morning to the middle-aged woman. He looked at her name tag, a blue name tag, and it read Margaret – his mother's name! It was at that moment that he realised his mother was there along with him. "From that moment, I had the best time. It was very healing, the cast member saying good morning to me…a single guy on the train."

One year Fr. George found himself doing a wedding just before he was leaving for Walt Disney World. And where were the newlyweds going to for their honeymoon? To Walt Disney World! "How often does a newly married couple meet up with their priest at Walt Disney World on their honeymoon?" He laughed.

Fr. George is also the sacramental minister at the University of Pittsburgh in Johnstown, Pennsylvania. Every week his parishioners wait for a Disney reference in his sermon. No matter what he preaches about, they will always sit there listening and smiling, wearing their Mickey Mouse and Elsa and Anna t-shirts. They stop him after mass just to talk "Disney." "There is a connection other than church" that he enjoys very much, he said.

Each year, Fr. George takes a group of parishioners with him on one of his visits to Walt Disney World. As he had been welcomed into the parish and into his parishioners' lives and hearts, he wanted to welcome them into a part of *his* life that holds a big place in *his* heart.

There are lessons to be learned there, Fr. George said. "If a corporation such as Disney, where everyone gets along and feels important, can do it, why can't we do that in the larger world? It *is* possible, we *can* do it. It's been proven. Humans can do it in 46 square miles."

"It doesn't matter whether you are pushing a broom or if you are a part of management. You are *all* part of the same family; and people hunger and thirst for this." And it's this connection – the Disney connection – that draws us back time and time again to the most magical place on earth.

GASTON'S LITTLE BELLE

"She was completely over the moon.
That made her holiday."

— EMMA JANE NAPIER

ANYONE WHO HAS READ MY books will have noticed the photo of Gaston and me on the back cover. He is one of my favourite characters, and he is my second favourite French guy, my husband being my first. And I told Gaston this when we met. Gaston is as conceited as he is charming, and most importantly, he makes me laugh at his most outrageous carrying-on's. When I had heard about the little lady in my next story, I knew that there might be some mischief afoot. However, Gaston, for once, was on his best behaviour if that is even possible when he met his little admirer Daisy, aka little Belle.

The Napier family, who are from the UK, developed their love for Disney a few years ago when James Napier's parents surprised the family with a trip to Walt Disney World. James had visited when he was a child and loved it, and his parents thought his family of five would enjoy it too. His wife Emma was not too fond of the idea initially. "I couldn't see the appeal for adults. I couldn't see what the fascination was." But when Emma walked through the gates, then she knew. "I stepped into the Magic Kingdom on that first day and that was it. I loved it."

The family found themselves back during their Easter break in 2016 when their youngest child Daisy, was 5 years old, son Devon was 9, and daughter Paige was 12. Daisy has always been a huge Beauty and the Beast fan, and she particularly liked the Beast. Her first experience at Hollywood Studios' *Beauty and the Beast* stage production had little Daisy in tears when the Beast died. Happily, enough, his spell was broken and he returned to the prince that he had always been, much to Daisy's relief. Although she didn't want him to turn into the prince she told her parents; she wanted him to remain as the Beast.

Because of Gaston's part in all of this, Emma thought Daisy would not be very fond of him at a meet-and-greet. However, Daisy still insisted on meeting him when she saw him.

The day that Daisy met Gaston for the first time, she was wearing a cute little blue dress with an apron, the one that Belle wears for her "everyday" look. When Emma had first spotted the dress, she knew she had to get it for her daughter. She had never seen anyone in it around the park before.

Daisy does not bring along regular clothes when she goes on vacation to Walt Disney World. She brings a bathing suit along with a suitcase full of princess dresses, a wardrobe designed for a princess! The addition of this new dress would be easy to pack along, Emma said.

Finally, it was Daisy's turn to meet Gaston, and she cautiously made her way up to him. And that did it. He absolutely loved her and asked this little Belle to marry him. Daisy said yes and what happened next was adorable. Gaston handed Daisy a red rose and took her by the hand to go for a stroll. Gaston brought little Belle to his tavern for some photographs and bought her one of the massive cinnamon buns they serve there. He asked her to wait there with her parents while he greeted the rest of his fans who were still in line waiting to meet him. About five minutes later he returned. They took some more photos together and then Gaston took little Belle out for another stroll around the courtyard. They parted ways soon after, albeit reluctantly. Daisy did not want him to go, but he had to. "She was completely over the moon. That made her holiday," Emma says.

Before the family returned to Walt Disney World during the summer of 2016, Emma tracked down Gaston online. She wanted to thank him for what he had done at Easter and tell him about how happy he had made Daisy. Emma mentioned that they would be going back for a visit. He asked if they could come around with Emma again. They set up a prearranged time so that Daisy would be his last guest in line. This way he could spend a little more time with her.

When Daisy walked over to him, the photographer and cast members could spot her from about a mile away Emma says. He remembered her right away to the thrill of a little Belle (and her family too). Daisy had brought along a gift for Gaston and gave it to him. It was a handheld mirror because she knew how much he loved looking at himself, and knew how gorgeous Gaston thought he was.

Gaston was really impressed with that. And he gave his little Belle another rose, a white one this time that sits next to the red one in her bedroom at home. Gaston took little Belle back over to his tavern once again and got her another cinnamon bun. They sat and had a good chat. "It was lovely." It was nice that he had remembered Daisy, and that he had given her a red rose and bought her a cinnamon bun the last time that he saw her, Emma said.

During Christmas of 2016, the Napier family found themselves back at Walt Disney World. Daisy wanted to show Gaston her most prized Christmas gift. It was a transforming dress that went from the everyday look of Belle's blue dress to a golden princess dress as you spin and detach the fastener. It had been specially made for Daisy by a man named Nephi Garcia, who is known as the "designer daddy." A friend of Emma's had put her in touch with him.

The Napiers were a little worried that he would not recognize her, and vice versa because Emma had not reached out to Gaston to let him know they were coming back for this visit. They tried to play it cool and not let on that anything was amiss, even though Devon and Paige were whispering to their parents that "that's not *the* Gaston." Emma said she stood there cringing and waiting for Daisy to reach him and realize that this wasn't "her Gaston."

Daisy had received two Gaston Tsum Tsums for Christmas and wanted to give him one. Emma agreed to the plan if Daisy did not mind parting with it. When it was her turn to see Gaston again, Daisy went up to him and handed him the Tsum Tsum. He didn't recognize what it was at first; he thought it was a little hamster. After a few moments, he realized that it was a Tsum Tsum of him! Little Belle asked Gaston if she could show him a bit of magic. She spun around, and her dress transformed before his eyes. He was really impressed and so was the crowd behind the Napiers who clapped and cheered. After her big reveal, little Belle had people asking *her* for an autograph. "It was hilarious. She felt like a celebrity."

When they returned home, Emma posted the video she had taken of Daisy on the Disney Facebook group, A Secret Group of Disney's Magical Theme Park Cast Members and Guests. There was quite a reaction to the post and it ended up being on a program called Right This Minute and on ABC News in the United States.

The family are annual pass holders and returned for a quick weeklong trip during the children's break from school in February of 2017. When James suggested that they go for a quick trip, Emma thought it was a bit too far to go for a week, using up two days for travel with the long flights each way. Once the family arrived however, it turned into a more relaxing visit than any previous trips to Walt Disney World. The parks were quiet, and although they crammed in a lot during that week, they didn't feel rushed. Their next trip was planned for Easter of 2017.

They never thought that they would be returning to Walt Disney World as much as they have. Emma's mother-in-law and father-in-law didn't quite expect them to "get the bug" quite as much as they have either.

Emma loves everything about Florida, and not just because of the obvious warmth and sunshine that it offers over the chilly rain of the UK. They have been to many beautiful places before, but they would rather go to Florida. "No matter where we go, we kind of wish we were at Walt Disney World."

The Napiers want to do as much of Walt Disney World as they can while their children are young and able to enjoy it together as a family.

It's the people, the friendly, polite cast members, and the magic of everything that has the family returning again and again. It makes Emma happy to see how genuinely happy Daisy, aka Belle, is when they are there. "It's unlike anywhere else."

After all, where else would little Belle be able to go to see her Gaston?

THE GIFT OF GOOFY,
THE MAGIC OF MICKEY

*"It was absolutely pure magic – I have
no other way to describe it."*

— *MIKEY JACOBS*

IT HAD ALWAYS BEEN HIS dream. Since he was a very little boy, Mikey dreamed about being a character at Walt Disney World. He wanted to make people laugh. He wanted to make them smile. He wanted to make them *happy*. You see, he got it. He understood the role and the value that the characters had. And in return for making others happy, he would feel loved, and he would be happy, too. He related to how everyone at Disney goes out of their way to be friendly. "I was drawn to that ideal. I just wish someone had tried to make me smile," he says about his childhood. Unfortunately, Mikey's child-hood was a bit of a rough one.

Mikey Jacobs grew up in Tampa, Florida, about a 45-minute drive to Walt Disney World. And on the occasion when his family would have company from out of state, they would visit the theme park, reinforcing Mikey's dream. He remembers looking back at the Magic Kingdom on the ferry ride and realizing that *that* was where he needed to be. "It's the one place I ever felt like a child."

Mikey's first job opportunity to work for Disney came as a cast member at a Disney store in Connecticut right out of high school. From there, he returned to Florida and began work in what used to be Mickey's Character Shop located at the old Disney Marketplace. He really loved it. It was different from working merchandise in the park. "It was much more laid back."

His love of interacting with guests found him in a position at the Polynesian Resort in what was called Guest Services back in the day, and is now called Guest Relations. It was here that Mikey fondly remembers feeling like he had a family at Disney. He loved his job there. At that time, cast members working Guest Relations sold tickets and shared and answered trivia. They also did some neat things for guests such as filling their room with balloons in celebration of an anniversary or sending up a treat if they noticed someone was having a bad day. Mikey decided that Guest Relations within the park was where he wanted to be. He began at City Hall in the Magic Kingdom. While working there, it was typical to be cross-trained for other jobs as well. In Mikey's case, this was as a tour guide and later, as a VIP tour guide.

He worked hard and learned every kid joke that he could. He became very good at making people laugh, and he enjoyed doing it immensely.

The best was yet to come for Mikey when a character opportunity became available. He was so excited! He auditioned and got the position, fulfilling his lifelong dream of being a character early in his life. He worked as a variety of characters including one of the "Fab Five" in the capacity of the one and only Goofy.

And he lived that dream for the next 20 years. Mikey shared that it didn't even feel like a real job; you were either playing with the guests or you were on a break. When he first started, there were no autograph books, digital cameras, or line-ups. Characters would just go out and play with the people.

As a character, you must encompass many roles and within those various roles, you have many, many experiences. Mikey recalled one occasion at the Character Spot at Epcot when there was a fellow by himself in line. There was no family around. As he got closer to meeting Goofy, the man stepped back and observed him interacting with the guests for about 10 minutes. Finally, the man came up, and he slipped something into the palm of Goofy's hand saying, "I have a friend that would have wanted you to have this." And then the man proceeded to hug and cry in Goofy's arms. Mikey could not see what the man had placed in his hand because he was only able to see straight ahead.

When Mikey went on his break, he looked at what it was that the man had given him.

It was a little pin that they give to military personnel who were POWs. Whoever the man had lost, was a big fan of Disney and an even bigger fan of Goofy, Mikey shares. "I cry every time I think about it. I still have the pin and it's one of my most prized possessions."

During another guest interaction, Mikey remembers an incredibly brave and strong albeit heart-broken woman. She told him that she had recently lost her husband and that they were in fact, supposed to be on the trip together. She requested a special photo of herself and Goofy to put on her mantle next to her husband's ashes. And then he just held the sobbing woman and she told Goofy that she loved him.

When he signed up, Mikey didn't realize how extensive the character department was. "As a character, we get to do things that you never think of doing." One of the positions a character could bid for was at Give Kids the World Village nearby.

On one of Goofy's visits there, he sat on the deathbed of a child. He was the last one to hug the child before he died. "That's an honour that I can't even tell you how much it means to me," Mikey says. He also shared that some of the kids don't make it to Walt Disney World so the characters go to see them at the village. And on many occasions, unfortunately, the kids pass away there.

Another boy that Mikey remembers had one dying wish: to meet and be held by Goofy. "And I happened to be *that* Goofy." The little boy was very fragile. Because of his delicate condition, he had had only a minimal amount of human contact. His mom showed Goofy how to hold her son and support his head.

And hold him he did.

Goofy held and rocked the little boy, who was nonverbal, back and forth and smiled. "I sat there at Give Kids the World and just hugged this kid. That's the kind of stuff that you just can't sign up for."

Goofy is aptly named because he is...well...goofy. But there is the other side of Goofy – the compassionate, healing, hugging side – the gifts of Goofy. Mikey got to experience all of this because of one January day in 1996 while working at Guest Relations in the Magic Kingdom that changed his heart forever. He had gone far in Guest Relations, but after that day he couldn't continue in that role. "It was absolutely pure magic – I have no other way to describe it."

In Mikey's own words, here is what happened that fate-filled day:

I have one moment that stands out above the rest. I was waiting for someone to ask me that question. It's the reason I left a good job as a VIP tour guide and moved to the character department.

I was working City Hall one day when two guests came in with two little girls. One was in a wheelchair, and the other one looked like she had just seen death. Both were cut and bruised and the one in the wheelchair had her arm in a cast. The two women were actually nurses from a hospital and were asking for a refund on the girls' tickets, something we avoided doing at all costs.

When I asked why, they told me the story. The two girls were with their mom and dad at Epcot, and on their way home, they got into a horrible car accident. The mother was beheaded in front of them. The father eventually died too, but the two girls didn't know that yet. They were from overseas and had no money or contact information for anyone they knew. They were bringing the tickets back to get the girls some much needed money to help get them back home. My heart absolutely sunk. If you had seen these girls, you'd know why. They were truly traumatized.

I refunded their tickets and got permission to be their private tour guide for the rest of the day (which they were not expecting). I walked with them to the VIP viewing area for the parade, which was as far as I could walk with them in the costume we used to wear at City Hall. I had to leave them there while I put on my VIP costume. On the way down, I pulled out every kid joke I could think of. I was a **REALLY** good tour guide (I helped write part of it) and I knew how to make kids smile. Nothing worked. These girls were too far gone for that.

I left them at the bridge to go change, walked backstage, and bawled my eyes out. I just had never seen something so horrible. I was truly affected and it was a terrible feeling of powerlessness not being able to fix the situation. When I came back. I brought them to get ice cream, take them on rides and stuff, but they never smiled, not once. The nurses were loving being there and were trying to get the girls into it but it just wasn't working. We went back to the bridge to watch the parade. It was there that I honestly saw true magic. Real magic, not BS.

I had called the parade department to let them know what was going on and set up a private meet-and-greet after the parade. As the parade was coming around Liberty Square, I told the girls that I had called Mickey and told him all about them. I told them that Mickey asked to meet them after the parade.

The little girl in the wheelchair smiled. "Really?" She asked.

My heart skipped. "Yes, really! He told me to tell you to look out for him in the parade and to follow the float back to City Hall."

The other girl smiled. "You mean right now?" She asked.

It had worked. They were talking. Not laughing, but at least talking. It was the first time I had heard them speak. Every single parade performer came up to on the bridge and told them to look out for Mickey. When Mickey's float came up, Mickey (who was attached to a pole at the top of the float) managed to turn his body sideways, look down at the girls, and point towards Main Street. That was all it took.

The girls were excited now. They had forgotten about death. They were lost in a magical world and I couldn't believe I was watching it unfold in front of my eyes. We followed that float all the way back to City Hall singing "Mickey Mania" the whole way back. Back then, City Hall used to have a VIP lounge behind the desk that was for privacy during difficult situations or to host celebrities. I took them in and showed them the book where all of the autographs were. They were eating it up.

The girl who was Mickey that day got off her float and without taking her head off, walked up to me backstage and said "Let's go." I walked in with Mickey behind me so I got to see the exact moment the girls met their new friend. They got shy, but Mikey was in control *now. Those girls met the **real** Mickey Mouse that day. Every single parade character stayed dressed to meet those girls. One by one they'd come in and play a bit and then leave. We were in that lounge for over an hour, which is hard to do after a parade. When Mickey finally said goodbye, I had two excited girls on my hands who couldn't stop smiling. They talked and talked and talked.*

We had a wonderful day after that, but what I remember most is when we walked by the rose garden, the older one said "Oh, my mommy loves roses! I mean..." and she stopped. I held out my hand and walked her to the gate, picked her up and put her on the other side and said "Pick one!" She looked happy as she picked out her favorite rose. She didn't say anything more and she didn't need to.

I said goodbye to the wonderful nurses and the wonderful girls, then walked backstage behind the train station. This time I didn't cry. It felt good to be a part of that. I realized that as much as I liked helping guests at City Hall, the true magic of Disney was in the character department.

So I auditioned, transferred, and never looked back. Thanks for letting me relive this. It was a special day for me.

Mickey, the iconic little mouse, is many things to many people. But what Mickey Mouse was to those little girls that day was *mighty*. He was both a *mighty* and *magical* presence that delivered two little girls from their unbelievable suffering, if only for a little while. And helping to ignite the magic of Mickey was a mighty man who had seen within these children, a version of his childhood self.

AFTERWORD

I CONTINUALLY COLLECT STORIES FOR the next *Positively Disney* book in this series. If you or anyone you know would like to share your story with me, please contact me at kimberley@ positivelydisney.com. I would love to hear from you!

Peace and pixie dust,

Kimberley

CONTRIBUTORS

Jennifer Baldovinos	Disney Sisters
Joe Bell	The Real Princess Tiana
Cheryl Biazzo	With a Little Help from Our Friends
Joe Biazzo	With a Little Help From Our Friends
Angelica Doria	Ms. Incredible
Mike Flynn	A Hope and a Dream
Abi Forrest	Tsum Tsums With Heart
Timothy Gill	Seeing Mickey
Fr. George Gulash	The Disney Connection
Dan Hartley	The Collector
Mikey Jacobs	The Gift of Goofy, The Magic of Mickey
Kevin-John Jobczynski	The Art of Life
Emmaline Johnson	Special Affects
Geoffrey Kanner	Marathon Man
Mell Mallin	Just Dance
Lisa Matters	My Goofy

Yesenia McCoy	Something Disney
Kylee McGrane	Power Princess
Kaley McLean	A Royal Proposal
Brenden McNeil	A Royal Proposal
Lou Mongello	You've Got a Friend in Me
Diane Myers	Happiness by Chance
Emma Jane Napier	Gaston's Belle
Andy Attwood Otto	The Ministry of Disney
Marissa Parks	Walking Warrior
Roberto Romero	Living the Dream
Basilio Santana	Seeing Mickey
Sara Slade	Disney Dreams for Everyone
Sophie Slade	Disney Dreams for Everyone
Toni Campitiello Smith	Toni's Time
Dora Speck	Dora's Dream
Nataly Pacifico White	Seeing Mickey
Amy Wyand	Misadventure
Michelle Young	Snow White's Gift
Mike Zevon	Double Acts of Kindness

ABOUT THE AUTHOR

KIMBERLEY BOUCHARD IS AN AUTHOR, educator, entrepreneur, podcaster, and speaker. She grew up watching the *Wonderful World of Disney* on television Sunday nights. Kimberley has visited Disneyland and Disneyland Paris, and is a frequent visitor to Walt Disney World. She loves all things Disney and unabashedly admits that Donald Duck is her guy. Originally from Canada, she now resides in the Seattle area with her husband, their three children, and various critters.